PSYCHOTHERAPY

AND PERSUASION

JOHN EATON

THE
DEEP
PRESS

In Memoriam

J. A. Eaton 1928-1991

Whose spirit of scepticism and curiosity is preserved here.

CONTENTS

INTRODUCTION

When I first set out to write about the ideas in this book my intention was to analyse the use of language patterns in the psychotherapy (e.g. metaphors, stories, suggestions, interpretations, reframes, analogies, etc.). My starting point was that it is these patterns we should study if we really want to understand how therapy works. As it turned out this idea was too simplistic although this book argues that a sophisticated version of this argument might be true.

I also wanted to explore other matters which were of interest to me as a practising psychotherapist at the time (late 1990s). What do therapists actually do when they are at work (as opposed to what they say they are doing)? Is therapy really a matter of persuasion, indoctrination and the exercise of power?

Side by side with this question is the issue of the scientific status of psychotherapy. Does effective therapy work because it is based on a science of the mind or is it that scientific claims make it more persuasive? Or is scientific method merely a chimera as it is so often in psychology and the other human sciences? More to the point: is there ever such a thing as a correct method in psychotherapy? If there is then we do not need to worry too much about those language patterns: following the right method is all that is required. My experiences as both researcher and as a practitioner had taught me to be sceptical about claims that one school or another had uncovered the 'right' way to do therapy where others had not. This scepticism has increased over time and is reflected in several places in this book.

As my research unfolded I became aware of the evolving use of discourse and conversation analysis in the social sciences in which texts and transcripts are analysed in order to reveal something about the way in which language is being used in stylised ways in different settings: medical, military, legal, scientific, and so forth. Some works using these methods on transcripts of therapeutic interviews had been published but I found much of this material unsatisfactory. Most of it had been published by non-therapists who seemed to have little notion of the interpersonal complexity of therapy sessions and whose analysis often led to simplistic claims that there was only one type of therapeutic discourse and that all therapy sessions followed the same linguistic patterns. A related difficulty is that it takes many hours of work just to analyse a single session of therapy, a fact which makes it difficult to generalise from any of the findings which emerge. A final difficulty is that there are many different styles of discourse analysis ranging from the history of a cultural practice to a minute analysis of a few minutes conversation.

It is certainly true that there exists a loose set of knowledge-practices which characterise psychotherapy and are embedded in the social history of Western societies. Some of these date all the way back to church confessionals. Others emerged from treatments for the insane in the late 18th century, from hypnosis in the 19th century, the rehabilitation of soldiers suffering from 'shell-shock' in World War I and from psychiatry. Evolving at last into a knowledge-practice in which clients present problems to experts that are assessed, analysed, understood, reworked and resolved in psychotherapy. All this sometimes leads to an argument in which therapy is seen as a way of overseeing and rehabilitating the mental health of citizens; a covert form of indoctrination in fact.

There are three things wrong with this argument. The first is that generalisations about what psychotherapy is for do not tell us much about what actually makes it work in detail. The second is that psychotherapy is not typically coercive; indeed it can be employed to emancipate clients from oppression. The final objection is a key argument in this book: that the course of therapy is nearly always unpredictable in practice.

It is a peculiarity of psychotherapy that books written about it rarely have much to say about clients' contributions to therapy. The emphasis is nearly always on the ideas, principles and methods of therapists. Or on what therapists should do to become better at it. Or on the different mental health problems for which it may be effective. Or else on the results that emerge from doing it. In short, the focus is on what therapists do rather than the game that is played out between two players.

Yet, as any practitioner will tell you, psychotherapy is hard to do and more often than not does not go the way that therapists intend. Those pesky clients have a way of misunderstanding, ignoring, or resisting what therapists have to say in the same way they will sometimes listen to, and put into practice, the ideas they find useful. They will also introduce material into the session that at first sight appears irrelevant, contradictory or even perverse and which takes therapy on a course which the therapist cannot foresee. In the same way clients (as is their right) can bring therapy to an abrupt end without explanation.

Psychotherapy is a contractual exchange between two or more people in which a service of some kind is offered. In this it bears a similarity to law and medicine. But unlike interviews with lawyers and medical doctors the content of the exchange - the material to be worked on - is offered up from the inner life of the client: her thoughts, sensations, emotions, judgments and memories; and from the source of her anxiety, depression or addictive behaviour, etc.

This subjective material forms the *content* of psychotherapy. The *process* of therapy evolves from the conversation therapists and clients have about it. During this exchange the therapist offers a series of constructions about the material - reflections, interpretations, suggestions, stories, analogies and metaphors, etc., which may, or may not, be followed by procedures which assist the client in some way. These conversations range in content from technical jargon at one end to everyday intuitions at the other.

Some therapists, it is true, are more persuasive than others. Sometimes this arises from their status: whether they are legends in the field, worthies festooned with honours, or best-selling authors peddling the latest fad. More usually it is because they are heard by clients as having something interesting to say which is relevant to their concerns.

The art of persuasion in psychotherapy ranges from straightforward indoctrination at one end to an open-ended discussion at the other. The established psychotherapies: psychodynamic therapy, cognitive-behaviour therapy, person-centred counselling, etc., come somewhere in the middle. The theories embodied in the approach generally set out a model of the mind, the causes of mental health problems, and the correct approach to take in curing them. Further principles underpin their therapeutic methods and the client is, covertly or not, introduced to these knowledge-claims during the course of psychotherapy. So much constitutes what I have called the 'rhetoric' of psychotherapy.

However, the use of method in psychotherapy is open to challenge both from critics of the method and from the clients upon whom they are foisted. In this book I have refrained from criticism of specific therapies as there already exists a large literature on this subject. My interest lies in uncovering the rhetoric of psychotherapy both on the written page and in the therapeutic interview.

It is a peculiar fact that many of the 20th century pioneers of psychotherapy were interesting, if not persuasive, writers. For this very reason we can approach their writings as works of literature and, in doing so, deconstruct the literary devices they used to construct their arguments. I have tried to do this principally in relation to the writings of Carl Rogers, Fritz Perls and Albert Ellis and to demonstrate how their written and spoken claims *about* therapy lead logically to the persuasive devices they employ *in* therapy using their 1965 interviews with 'Gloria' as examples.

These interviews lead back to the most important argument in this book: that so long as psychotherapy seeks to be a conversation of sorts (as opposed to a monologue) then it cannot escape the restrictions that the rules of conversation place on interpretation. On the basis that clients accept what therapists have to say in the first place, as having something relevant, truthful and trustworthy to convey to them, those same arguments still need to be understood, digested and accepted. I argue that this happens less often than observers of psychotherapy might think. Within the give-and-take of conversation clients will exercise the right to dismiss, clarify, counter-argue or else accept the offerings of the therapist. However, even here things may go awry, for the client's interpretation of the opportunities before him may differ from that of his therapist. It is this constant play of interpretation, counter-interpretation, synthesis and re-synthesis that make therapeutic conversations what they are.

Assuming that an intervention is accepted the client still has to find a use for it for psychotherapy is, at bottom, a pragmatic enterprise which aims at results. And, here, too, the course of a psychotherapy may take a very different direction from the one the practitioner might have hoped. New ideas are frequently misunderstood or misapplied in practice. The new idea, or technique, accepted with enthusiasm in one session turns out to be unworkable or to have been quietly forgotten by the time the next session comes around. Sometimes quite promising advances are overtaken by unforeseen accidents in the client's life. It may also happen that reported successes owed little to anything the therapist may have said or done but to changes taking place elsewhere in the client's life which leave them better placed to go forward without further help.

For all these reasons psychotherapy can never be a formal, repeatable method which applies to all people in the same fashion. Still less can it be a science. It will always be a conversational art - and nor, I argue, should it ever be anything else.

At the close of this book I turn to hermeneutic philosophy in order to deepen the discussion in four different ways:

a) why over-reliance on method in psychotherapy may end not in the health of the client but in adherence to the method

b) how all interpretations are prejudicial: a factor which must be understood before employing them in order to develop a genuine dialogue with the client

c) that all genuine attempts to understand the position of another take the form of a conversation, in which the to-and-fro of interpretation and counter-interpretation take us a few steps forward to 'a fusion of horizons' in which we grasp something new and unforeseen about the other

d) that there are no final truths about any human being or any state of affairs and the course of psychotherapy should reflect this premise.

Note

Psychotherapy and Moral Inquiry was originally a paper published in *Theory and Psychology* in 2002. It is included in an Appendix as its arguments are an extension to some of the main ideas in this book.

PSYCHOTHERAPY AS SCIENCE

THE PROBLEM OF PSYCHOTHERAPY - THE SCIENTIFIC
PROJECT - THE CASE OF ARNOLD LAZARUS - PROCESS &
OUTCOME RESEARCH - WILHELM REICH ON THERAPY

*What science can there be when everything is vague
and depends on an endless variety of
circumstances, the significance of which becomes
manifest all in a moment, and no one can tell when
that moment is coming?*

Tolstoy, 1978. War and Peace.

The problem of psychotherapy

The problem of psychotherapy might be
summarised like this: how is personal change generated from talk? And what is the precise nature of
the expertise which achieves such results? Such
questions, baldly stated, do not admit of straightfor-

ward answers. One reason for this is that some answers open up as many new questions as those resolved. This particularly applies to the attempt to identify and isolate the factors at work in therapeutic interviews. It applies still more to the texts in which theorists set out their claims. Such texts, typically, offer a psychology which underpins clinical practice, or sets out rules for doing therapy, or they offer readings of therapeutic interviews designed to be exemplary. These materials can be guides to therapeutic practice intended to be reproduced by student therapists in their own work. But they can also form a prison.

The Oxford English Dictionary defines 'psychotherapy' as referring to any treatment for 'disorders of the mind' a definition which hints at a medical origin for the practice. While psychotherapy does indeed reveal many traces of its descent from medical practices these traces are not constitutive. Psychotherapists, for the most part, are less concerned with pathology, diagnosis and prescription than with the way in which the self came to be constructed (Clare, 1976: 53-4) or else with its future direction. Although it is true that some psychiatric institutions within the UK now offer psychotherapy to clients this could be viewed largely as a supplement to their work rather than as an integral part. Even so a hard-and-fast distinction between psychiatry and psychotherapy will not be pressed; the differences lie across a spectrum with biochemical treatments at one end and purely conversational methods at the other with much else in between. Insofar as psychiatrists offer talking cures their work falls within the scope of this inquiry.

Some forms of therapy are not restricted to just talk but may include visualisation, role play, the keeping of diaries, painting, movement & dance, sexual techniques, acting-out, physical massage, behavioural tasking and hypnosis, all of which are either adjuncts to the main business of talk or are themselves the basis of the therapeutic treatment. While this welcome multiplicity is acknowledged work of this kind must fall outside the scope of this work which is restricted to the examination of conversational and textual practices. Psychotherapy as talk and text forms the material for discussion throughout this work if only for reasons of economy and space.

The newcomer to the field cannot fail to be struck by the sheer number of therapies that are available. One book (Herink, 1980) has the sub-title 'The A to Z Guide to more than 250 different therapies in use today' and gives the impression of a field marked by a chaotic proliferation of techniques which spin off endlessly, and fortuitously, in addition to mainstream practices. Such a divergence of approach leads to the problem of whether there is a unitary field of psychotherapy which can be studied or (if not) what could constitute the subject of our investigation. To answer this question we might ask: how many psychotherapies could there be? Although over 250 are listed in the work referred to above many of those described are: nearly synonymous ('Existential-Humanistic Psychotherapy' & 'Existential Group Therapy'), overlap considerably in content (e.g. 'Rational-Emotive Therapy' & 'Cognitive Therapy'), refer to techniques rather than therapies (e.g. 'Bibliotherapy'), are perspectives ('Feminist Therapy'; 'Christian Therapy'), or not recognised psychotherapies at all ('Aikido'). The list of discrete approaches is thus considerably shorter, perhaps 20-30 if we eliminate the anomalies listed. Another introductory work (Harper, 1959) lists 36 kinds of therapy but ten of these are psychodynamic approaches. Kovel (1976) meanwhile lists 21 separate therapies under four general headings: analytical, humanistic, group therapy, and behavioural-directive. The United Kingdom Council for Psychotherapy, one of the main registering bodies in that country, lists 75 member organisations nearly all offering their own training courses in different versions of the therapeutic enterprise. The organisations are listed in eight main sections: Analytical (i.e. Jungian) Psychology, Behavioural-

Cognitive, Experiential-Constructivist, Family/Systemic therapy, Humanistic, Hypnotherapy, Psychoanalytic and Child Psychotherapy. The difficulty in fixing the exact number of approaches which are both independent of each other and recognisable as therapies suggests a problem for researchers and practitioners alike in defining just what activities are to count as doing psychotherapy. It indicates, indirectly perhaps, that a host of different social practices, ideas and techniques are gathered under the umbrella of 'psychotherapy'. Yet, it would seem, there is little concern amongst practitioners themselves that the profession they follow is not based on any agreed body of ideas. In fact many of those in practice are eclectic in their approach and, we are told (Smail, 1983) concern themselves little, if at all, with theoretical justifications for their work or with scientific research which seeks to provide evidence, one way or the other, for the effectiveness of psychotherapy itself, either in the generic or for one particular approach over another.

Since a unified field of inquiry seems to be lacking then this work will assume the existence of disunity; the fragmentary nature of the discipline will be understood as a given. This in fact constitutes an advantage in one sense for it enables the enquiry to switch from considerations of theoretical validity to issues of practical action. That is we can ignore what psychotherapy 'really' is and look instead at how therapists are doing what they consider is psychotherapy; how that is, they are constructing the object in view

The scientific project

The history of psychotherapy, like that of psychology, is replete with attempts to found the discipline on scientific principles (Ellenberger, 1994). This, historically, has taken one of three forms. The first has been to found the practice of psychotherapy on discoveries which have elsewhere been shown to be scientifically valid; we will call this 'the scientific project'. The second has been to find evidence that a therapeutic approach is scientifically established if it consistently produces a quantifiable and significant reduction of observable symptoms; this we will refer to as outcome research. The third, that psychotherapy is valid if it employs techniques that consistently and quantifiably produce desirable changes in personal function; we will refer to this as process research.

A famous attempt of the first type was made by Freud right at the start when, in 1895, he drew up a *Project For A Scientific Psychology* (Freud, SE I: 295-397) which was to establish the still nascent practice of psychoanalysis (a term not invented until the following year) as a 'natural science' (op. cit. p295) on a reductionist programme of psychology in which all mental functions were reduced to psycho-physical forces working to Fechner's basic principle of energy conservation. In Freud's view of the Unconscious at that time its contents were filled with repressed wishes connected up to pieces of libido. The exact quantity of libido attached to each repressed desire could be measured, in principle, from the severity of the psychosomatic symptoms which resulted. Psychoanalytic interpretations which uncovered forbidden wishes would be vali-dated by their success in removing those symptoms, while the method itself was justified by its basis in known laws of neurological functioning. Best of all psychoanalysis as a mode of treatment would be unassailable as even therapeutic failures would prove the underlying theory correct, in rather the same way that botched experiments indicate, by default, the (unfollowed) correct procedure. Unsuc-cessful treatments would be attributed to the failings of the therapist who would then be alerted to the need for further supervision.

In this paradigmatic mode of justification for what he was doing Freud shows himself to have been a child of his time for it had been the great success of the natural sciences (in which he was originally trained) in the nineteenth century which had

encouraged the application of positivism to such
disciplines as economics, sociology and psychology.
The reasons for which Freud abandoned the project
and chose not to publish this work during his life-
time are instructive for the very issue we are
discussing here. The first was due to the insuperable
difficulty in explaining how mechanical forces
repressed both pleasurable and unpleasurable
sensations and which resulted also in the wide
variety of symptom reactions against trauma actually observed, from severe neurosis, to hysteria, or
complete absence of pathology (Sulloway, 1980:
113-131). Hence the concrete reactions of clients
seemed to be just as much a result of personality
and circumstance as of neurological action; their
manifestation a matter of personal interpretation as
of neurology.

The second reason was that the projected theory of
mind outlined in the Project was incompatible with
Freud's interpretative method as it then stood. In
particular, Freud was unable to account for the
psycho-physical status of parapraxes, psychosomatic symptoms, jokes, dreams and amnesias
outside their conditions of interpretation (Gay,
1988: 80). The practical enterprise he was engaged
on sought to unravel the unconscious meaning of
these phenomena and the trace operations required
to perform such a reading relied on a kind of

hermeneutic appraisal rather than a positivistic one. As such the work of interpreting such materials turned out to be a specifically conversational affair and the problem of equating the meaning of symptoms to fixed quantities of energy circulating in the nervous system proved insuperable although Freud retained the hope that one day it could be done.

Thus the actual work of psychoanalysis (as opposed to Freud's theory of the mind) turned out to be discursive rather than scientific in a way which became fateful for the discipline as a whole. It retains this characteristic as a conversational practice from then until now, a feature identified by Bakhtin, in 1927:

The motifs of the unconscious revealed during psychoanalytic sessions by means of the method of 'free association' are verbal reactions of the client, as are all other habitual motifs of consciousness. They are different one from the other, so to speak, not by any generic distinction of their being, but only by their content, that is ideologically....What is reflected in these verbal utterances is not the dynamics of the individual soul but the social dynamics

of the interrelations of doctor and client.
(Bakhtin, quoted in Todorov, 1984: 31).

What was an obstacle for Freud in grounding his
Scientific Project continues to throw up hazards for
theorists a century later: the problem of making
good general claims concerning the workings of the
psyche on the back of conversational materials
taken from interviews with single individuals. Freud,
at least, was astute enough to realise that this task
would not be a straightforward one and so he post-
poned it. In the meantime, he conceived psychoanalysis to be a method of inquiry into unconscious
processes, which, based on concrete interactions
with clients, could at least achieve idiographic
results. Psychoanalysis, while not yet a science in the
same way that physics was, had at least taken the
first, necessary, steps towards scientific legitimacy.
For this reason Freud attached considerable weight
to his published case histories. In Freud's accumulation of case results, and his willingness to modify his
theories in the light of them, the movement began
to build a body of tacit knowledge which could be
passed on to its trainees. From the outset, then,
Freud and his followers rode a kind of rhetorical
tandem in which case descriptions pointed up the
sure results of the therapeutic techniques, while
theoretical speculation unravelled the true nature of

the Unconscious which the therapy was (in some way yet to be demonstrated) held to modify. Each set of materials provided complementary discourses without their ever actually meeting on the same ground. This separation between the different kinds of evidence for psychoanalysis keeps at bay the problem of explaining how one kind is to be operationalised in terms of the other but at the cost of creating uncertainty in that it keeps the methodic claims of psychoanalysis in limbo. Meanwhile, actual encounters between therapists and clients remain, as Bakhtin realised, a matter of verbal and social interactions.

In his failure to resolve the split between his theory of mind and clinical practice and complete his project Freud presided over a breach which has become characteristic of the field. The gap between foundational knowledge (of the psyche) and tacit knowledge (of how to treat clients) continues to exist and for that reason psychotherapy is open to the suspicion that it achieves its effects not because it has access to the truth of the subject but by the influence the therapist brings to bear on the client. Since the therapist's inferences about what is going on in the Unconscious (or the nervous system, the mind, the self, etc.) are passed on to the client it follows that successful treatment may well be due to persuasion rather than to the treatment method.

Wittgenstein's attack on the scientific ideals of psychoanalysis, on these grounds and others, was all the more telling for the fact that he considered himself 'a disciple of Freud' (Wittgenstein, 1966: 41) and saw similarities between his own method in philosophy and that of psychoanalysis. To put it simply he saw psychoanalysis as bad science but good rhetoric:

Freud is constantly claiming to be scientific. But what he gives is speculation - something prior even to the formation of a hypothesis... there is no way of showing that the whole result of analysis may not be 'delusion'. It is something which people are inclined to accept and which makes it easier for them to go certain ways: it makes certain ways of behaving and thinking natural for them. They have given up one way of thinking and adopted another. Wittgenstein, 1966: 44-45)

For Wittgenstein psychoanalysis has no moorings in scientific method and this being so we can never be sure that therapeutic results are not due to the speculative skills of the therapist. More tangibly, this type of psychotherapy achieves its results not by disentangling from the Unconscious real wishes charged with affect but by providing clients with opportunities with which they can reconfigure the meaning of their personal history.

In the light of criticisms such as these revisionists have argued that psychoanalysis is a method which uncovers semantic significance rather than causal origins (see, for example, Rycroft, 1968; Storr, 1979). In this perspective it is not traumas which cause pathology it is the interpretation of an event as 'traumatic' by the sufferer; a signification that might even be a product of therapy itself. If, therefore, psychotherapy is an exchange which results in a change to the client's mode of interpretation then it is discursive rather than analytic. That is, it does not uncover new facts but new meanings; old facts are reframed in terms of new interpretations which lend themselves to more fruitful forms of social and personal action.

Since Freud other attempts have been made to reduce psychotherapy to a naturalistic science. One such is Behaviour therapy and its successors (e.g. Cognitive-Behavioural therapy), in which the repertoire of techniques offered to clients is grounded in Learning theory and, later on, in Social-Cognitive theory (Nelson-Jones, 1995). From the outset Behavioural therapy was driven along by an anti-psychoanalytic argument. As psychoanalysis was (alleged

to be) unscientific then the need arose for a form of
therapy taken directly from laboratory work. As
Joseph Wolpe, an early advocate of Behaviour therapy, puts it:

> Before the advent of behaviour therapy,
> psychological medicine was a medley of
> speculative systems and intuitive methods.
> Behaviour therapy is an applied
> science....Therapeutic possibilities radiate
> from the uncovering of the lawful relations
> of lawful organismic processes. (Wolpe,
> 1973: xi)

Here 'applied science' is contrasted with 'intuitive
methods' and the 'possibilities' which are to be elaborated in the book are passively spun off by the
wheel of law-constrained organic processes. Note
the use of the passive/neutral case as laws are
uncovered: such presentations are characteristic of
'empiricist repertoires' in positivist arguments
(Gilbert & Mulkay, 1984) in which investigators are
seen as passively noticing natural processes as these
unfold before them. The repetition of the word
'lawful' emphasises the regularity of these processes;
an order not easily to be attributed to the subjective
preferences of the observer. It also sets up an

unfavourable contrast with the 'medley' of speculations which existed prior to the unveiling of biolog-
ical laws.

As was the case for Freud's Project Wolpe's ambi-
tion was for psychotherapy to be founded on biol-
ogy. Problematically, it is uncertain what knowledge
of organic laws will do to aid the student in understanding how to carry out therapy on human
beings. For example, an important principle in
behaviour therapy is Wolpe's Law of Reciprocal
Inhibition (Wolpe, 1958) in which the evocation of
one response (e.g. relaxation) will decrease the
strength of an antagonistic response (e.g. tension)
thereby weakening the bond between the latter and
the stimulus. However, much of the evidence for
this principle was gathered from laboratory tests on
cats given a conditioning for anxiety by means of
electric shocks and then de-conditioned by the elici-
tation of feeding responses. Yet, practically, it is
included within a treatment programme for
humans in which the responses elicited are
complex, qualitatively different, and at several
removes from conditioned reflexes (e.g. assertive-
ness, self-reinforcement, desensitisation, etc.).

Such accounts rely on an authorising chain in
which each link in the argument is legitimised by
the one before. Thus a communion with nature ('or-
ganismal processes') establishes experimental find-

ings. These give rise to laws of behaviour and these, in turn lead to observations concerning human learning. Finally, such laws are held to form the basis for an effective type of psychotherapy. But it is just this last link which is problematic in three different senses. Firstly, how can practitioners be sure that clients have achieved their cures from learning principles? And given that therapists cannot control environmental variables in the same way that laboratory investigators can, how can we eliminate the placebo effect and other influences on the client? More fundamentally, how are observers to know whether 'learning' in therapy is equivalent to the kind of learning elicited from animal trials?

Arnold Lazarus: 'It depends'

We now turn to some extracts from an interview with the founder of Multimodal therapy. These illustrate much of what has been said so far about the conundrums which result from textual claims that psychotherapy should, or could, be an applied science. Arnold Lazarus was at one time a student and then a colleague of Wolpe's and was influential in fostering interest in Behaviour therapy in the USA and elsewhere during the 1960s. During the 1970s he became one of the originators of what is now called Cognitive-Behavioural Therapy. He is well known for his eclecticism and in Multi-modal

Therapy (Lazarus, 1989) a range of Cognitive-Behavioural and other techniques are deployed in order to match the client's presentational style at assessment. Lazarus is notorious for his use of the oxymoron 'the authentic chameleon' (Dryden, 1991: 17) to describe his preferred therapeutic style, asserting that therapists should be ready to ditch their acquired principles and be ready to change their strategy to suit the situational demands posed by the client.

The interview from which this extract is taken is entitled 'A Dialogue with Arnold Lazarus: 'It Depends'.' (Dryden, 1991). Fairly early on in the transcript Lazarus tells us that the 'most viable' theories of psychotherapy 'are those that can be refuted' by experiments (Dryden, 1991: 7). For that reason social learning theory is his favourite since it is based on laboratory research and so is best positioned to 'explain what happens clinically' (ibid p8). Even so, he is happy 'to leave the theorising to others' since he is an 'empiricist' with an interest in the practical application rather than the abstract hypothesis. This is one reason for his eclectic, free-wheeling, approach to therapy:

....because people are unique and different, one has often to fly by the seat of one's

> pants to invent things at the spur of the
> moment, and draw upon methods that are
> less than immaculately researched, and
> quite often develop principles of one's own
> in the consulting room. (p27)

Although theories of psychotherapy need to be experimentally testable their operational worth is contingent upon the demands of the moment. The result is that methods may be used which fall short of ideal standards of research in the laboratory. Use of the litote 'less than immaculately' points up a contrast between the ideal and the mundane. That something is less than immaculate means something closer to poor - although this is not said. Later in the interview it emerges that Lazarus uses techniques which, he says, are 'frowned upon' (p26), 'off the beaten track' (p27) or from 'not acceptable' schools of thought (p28). The reasons for this are due to the 'unique', diverse, ways in which clients participate in therapy. This leads to an apparent contradiction in that the authentic chameleon chooses both 'pseudo-scientific' methods and 'well-researched laboratory-based' techniques. This incongruity is resolved on pragmatic grounds: even where one does not use the scientifically tested procedure the results can still be 'salubrious' (p29). Even so a good therapist must avoid just collecting a 'pot-pourri of notions, concepts and ideologies' because this does not provide a body of 'cohesive or coherent knowledge' (p54). Technical eclectics can only avoid this pitfall provided they have been endowed with 'a systematic scientific grounding....and an understanding of social learning theory.' (ibid), a claim which still does not answer the question: what is the connection between theoretical knowledge and clinical practice? The 'biggest problem that all clinicians face' (p30) is how to secure 'compliance' from the client. For this reason treatment selection is 'not at all mechanical' (p29) but a matter of sound judgement as each technique must be accommodated to the 'idiosyncratic properties of each individual so that client and therapist can form a liaison that can promote adherence or compliance' (ibid.). For all these reasons 'psychotherapy is both a science and an art' (p30).

Lazarus's interview answers address an issue which will be familiar to many practising therapists, particularly those newly qualified: how is a classroom training to be adapted to live interview conditions? Therapeutic interviews are liable to take unforeseen turns: the presenting problem fits into no category encountered before; the 'tried and tested' intervention that worked well before fails miserably now; the client becomes unaccountably upset or confused; a considered interpretation is rejected derisively; flippant asides are taken with the utmost seriousness; when we are too procedural we risk alienation, when too complaisant the work goes nowhere. Much of the live work of psychotherapy seems far from the training one received in diagnostics, assessment routines, personality theory, therapeutic principles and even from the demonstrations watched on video-tape. What in class sounded like an exact science seems more like an incomplete set of rules-of-thumb in practice which, too often, require further watering-down if they are to inform what one actually does. Lazarus, unusually and creditably, has made this problem a focus for his claims. He tells us of his readiness to discard ideas and follow his pragmatic sense of where the client can best go to achieve benefit. But in seeking to trace these ad hoc practices back to a 'systematic scientific grounding' (p54) a question of priority arises. Do therapeutic interventions follow from the theory, or is the theory called in to explain why the selection was made after the fact? A close reading of the text favours the latter as Lazarus tells us that he in fact uses theory to 'explain what I do' (p26). If that is the case then the link between scientific theories and clinical practice is little more than a marriage of convenience.

We may note that talk of science occurs in contexts where Lazarus is arguing for the worth of Multimodal therapy and where he is disparaging rival forms of treatment as incoherent or unsound. But talk of a free use of techniques on an 'it depends' principle occurs most often where Lazarus is discussing what he actually does in the consulting room. Thus while the 'scientific' vocabulary goes with the topic of validity, the pragmatic one rides along with the clinical issue. The two are reconciled later on in the interview when Lazarus turns to the question why 'the purely scientifically minded people failed to see the value' in his pragmatic innovations (p108):

There is an interesting fact about the field of behaviour therapy. Many of the leading figures are themselves not therapists. For example Hans Eysenck, who has been a leading spokesperson for behaviour therapy, has never treated a client in his life. There is an enormous difference in my opinion between academics or pure researchers who sit in ivory towers or in sealed laboratories, versus those of us who are in the trenches, you might say, dealing with the battlefront conditions of client care and responsibility. What was also interesting was that many a researcher who began clinical practice was humbled

> within a year or two and began to talk far
> differently from their stereotypic rigid ways
> when they were pure researchers. (ibid).

Science here is equated with the experimental
conclusions on which behaviour therapy is
(allegedly) founded. Multimodal therapy is clearly
distinguished from this, as is Lazarus's own practice.
The justification for Lazarus's innovations then,
rests on his experience 'in the trenches'. 'Pure'
research, leading to 'stereotypic rigid' opinions, is
only possible so long as one stays in a 'sealed laboratory' and never actually does any clinical work. We
are then offered a vignette in which 'many a
researcher' found their opinions changing once they
were involved in doing therapy. The metaphors of
'ivory towers' and 'sealed' laboratories work to
distinguish between battle-hardened veterans such
as Lazarus himself and the 'pure' but practically
naive approach of the academic.

The gap between theory and practice requires
rhetorical work if the 'scientific' therapist is to
present his case plausibly. A safe way of retaining
coherence is to fall back on a narrative style of
proof. Many of Lazarus's answers in the interview
are built around brief descriptions of cases he has
encountered. He, like Freud, has an Aristotelian

approach to proof: anecdotal evidence is held up as the exemplary case. Instead of statistical measures which summarise the relation between technique choice and clinical success, or theoretical approach and wholesale outcomes, case histories are adumbrated as an example of the real-life problems novices must overcome amidst the complexities of the therapeutic process. In the meantime scientific credentials are retained via reliance on the weight of accumulative results (Freud) or the claim that therapeutic techniques, if they are to be effective, must be ultimately explicable by clinicians in terms of their prior scientific training (Lazarus).

Process & outcome research: all must have prizes

We now turn to examine another positivist project for psychotherapy. Here the aim has been either to establish the best type of therapy measured by its results (outcomes) or to identify the specific things therapists do which make therapy work (processes). A key feature of scientific method is, of course, to isolate a causal variable and then to measure the effects of manipulating this on some other variable. Applied to psychotherapy research this principle has yielded many thousands of outcome and process research studies in which researchers seek to isolate curative factors in therapy.

An outcome study compares the rate of cure between two therapeutic approaches, or between a single approach and a control group. A process study measures changes in clients' behaviours following (isolable) events in therapeutic interviews. What both have in common is that a common feature of psychotherapy is identified as a factor in change (e.g. theoretic orientation, technique, conversational manoeuvre, etc.) and the effects of that variable when present are measured against the effects of alternative conditions in which that variable is absent. One implicit aim in both kinds of studies is to identify those factors which make psychotherapy effective and, having done so, to found the discipline on a scientifically established set of base procedures. From this investigators would then be able to go on to construct a manual of procedures and offer it to trainees confident that everything in the manual was a tried and tested, valid mode of treatment. If such variables can be linked to the theoretical model employed, and these in turn are shown to be effective in treatment, then one might also be able to claim, indirectly and pragmatically, that the theory on which the approach is founded has been shown to be scientifically validated.

Eysenck's seminal (1952) paper: '*The effects of psychotherapy: an evaluation*' was among the first to emerge. Eysenck took issue with the claims of psychoanalysis to be an effective cure and denied that it was so by comparing the rate of recovery in clients receiving treatment with spontaneous remission rates in no-treatment groups. He concluded that therapeutic recovery rates in neurotics receiving psychotherapy were, at best, no better than remission rates in clients who were in hospital or on a waiting-list. In a further (1966) study he followed up this attack with further claims that military and civilian patients treated by psychotherapy were no better off than untreated controls and that the only valid psychological treatments were those based on learning theory.

In point of fact there are very few quantitative studies which conclusively demonstrate that specific psychotherapies are effective in a general way. And there are many which point in the other direction. At present Cognitive-Behaviour Therapy (CBT) is attracting the most research attention here in the UK given that it is now the most commonly funded therapy in the British National Health Service. However no randomised clinical trials have so far demonstrated conclusively that CBT achieves any long-term improvement in patients. A 2005 survey of eight clinical trials carried out in Scotland on CBT in the previous twenty years showed that any initial improvement in symptoms had disappeared after two years and that more intensive or longer-term CBT made no difference in cases of anxiety or psychosis compared to control groups (Durham et. al., 2005).

Eysenck's claims, as well as the value of quantitative studies in general, have been frequently attacked (see, for example, Bergin & Lambert, 1978). Some critics assert that quantitative analysis rather misses the point: one analogy (Oatley, 1984) given is that it is like doing a follow-up study on the benefits of friendship, with friends to number up the gains from their relationships with each other, while researchers adjust the figures in order to allow for 'drop-outs' or terminated friendships. Thus Eysenck's claims are undermined on the grounds that his analysis misses the essentially qualitative nature of the therapeutic experience. This analogy suffers from two weaknesses, however. The first is that there is nothing to stop psychologists from researching friendship in this way, odd as it might seem to outsiders (and some do - see Aronson, 1976). The other is that it misses the essentially professional nature of psychotherapy. While we might be reluctant to charge a fee for friendship, psychotherapists do. Thus there is an implicit contractual claim to some sort of professional expertise for which a fee is justified.

Some researchers have attempted to defend the

worth of their versions of psychotherapy and refute Eysenck by offering quantitative studies of their own which purport to show that their own brand of therapy, or psychotherapy in general, is significantly effective, and far more so than the placebo effect or spontaneous remission rates. Bergin & Lambert (1978) and Smith, Glass & Miller (1980) amongst others have shown that therapy (including not just Psychoanalysis but also Cognitive-Behavioural therapy, Client-centred therapy, Transactional analysis, Gestalt therapy, etc.) is more effective than no-therapy conditions. The Smith, Glass and Miller study includes some comparisons between the insight psychotherapies and behavioural therapies in which the latter, while coming off best in outcome studies for specific anxiety disorders does not (it is claimed) have an advantage over other approaches when all classes of disorder are taken into account.

However, one result of these studies has called into question their paradoxical conclusions and, therefore, their intrinsic worth. For example, the Smith, Glass & Miller review concluded:

> Different types of psychotherapy (verbal or behavioural; psychodynamic, client-centred, or systematic desensitisation) do

> not produce different types or degrees of
> benefit. (Smith, Glass & Miller, 1980: 184).

But if all therapies have been found to be effective
(albeit, for some, for a restricted range of problems)
then a number of fresh heads arise on the
Eysenckian hydra. An example is the 'Dodo effect'
(Luborsky & Singer, 1975; Stiles et al, 1986) named
after the Dodo in *Alice in Wonderland* who declares,
following the caucus race, that 'All have won and all
must have prizes.' The paradox (Stiles et al, 1986) is
that each particular form of therapy is based on
very different procedures and theoretical constructs
from the others, and yet (it is claimed) each is
equally effective. But if this is so, what makes 'therapy' therapeutic? What is to distinguish the worth
of one particular piece of work over another if this
cannot (conclusively) be shown to rest on the theory
and method from which it takes its bearings?

A related difficulty lies in deciding whether
psychotherapists in clinical practice actually do
follow the therapeutic model in which they were
trained, or to which they publicly subscribe (leaving
aside the great number of experienced therapists -
possibly the majority - who are eclectic in orientation). Clearly, if the therapeutic session does not
mirror the procedural rules in which the therapist

was originally trained, or which she claims to follow, then comparisons between the outcome of that session and outcomes taken elsewhere are meaningless. Yet this is precisely what appears to happen:

Tape recordings of therapeutic sessions reveal that what therapists actually do differs significantly from what attempts to formalise their practices would suggest they do. (Holmes & Lindley, 1989: 29).

It follows that it cannot be the formal principles on which each model is based which can be the key to therapy; the locus of cure must lie elsewhere. As we saw from the Lazarus interview, there seems to be a loose relation between theory and practice which is resolved by calling upon pragmatic methods of proof - what appears to work well - rather than upon science.

The inconclusive findings from outcome research led to a shift in attention away from this to process research in the 1980s. Formerly, this had been the dominant type of analysis in the 1950s but was generally discounted as too complex and costly to be worthwhile. Even so Fiedler was amongst the first to conclude that the length of professional experience acquired by the psychotherapist was a greater guide to therapeutic outcomes than the theoretical approach adopted (Fiedler, 1950). This finding was later on supported by Garfield (1980) and Orlinsky & Howard (1987) who in both cases drew further attention to the influence of non-specific factors such as personal warmth, encouragement, supportive listening and empathy while Sloane et. al. (1975) found that experienced behavioural therapists were just as likely to develop rapport with their clients as experienced psychoanalysts were to offer covert, or even overt, reinforcement. Other factors that have been cited as key variables in exciting beneficial outcomes, include trust (Sloane et al, 1975); empathy (Truax & Mitchell, 1971); social support (Orlinsky & Howard, 1987); insight (Garfield, 1980); the therapeutic alliance (Luborsky et al, 1985); desensitisation (Rachman & Wilson, 1980); reinforcement & self-efficacy (Bandura, 1984); as well as the placebo effect (Frank, 1973; Wilkins 1984). Thus it would seem that, regardless of their testified approach, skilful therapists worked in similar ways and their skills had more to with clinical experience and tacit knowledge than with the methods they had been taught.

The complexities of process research are shown up by the problems which arise in deciding what is to count as a communicative event. This could range from a brief pause in the conversation to an extended narrative which is dropped and taken up again over a few dozen interviews. A further problem concerns the quantity and depth of information to be analysed. Is the researcher to carry out a micro-analysis of brief turns in the talk, or a macro-analysis of the gross results from hundreds of interviews? How much attention is to be paid to non-verbal cues such as intonation, pause and gesture? An idea of the complexity involved in such analyses is shown by Labov & Fanshel's (1977) work in which a fifteen-minute segment from one psychotherapy session took them nine years of open-ended analysis. They refer to the omission of video-taped data in their analysis as a weakness but also point out that research procedures which included such information would make 'the problem of data reduction very severe.' (Labov & Fanshel, 1977: 355).

If outcome research and process research taken separately are flawed some researchers have argued that those flaws are best overcome by doing both together. On this plan outcome research checks for the best approach while process research teases out what those 'best' approaches do that works well. These 'multi-directional' studies typically bring together groups of clients with the same presenting problem, each assigned to experimental & control groups, with therapists matched on key variables (e.g. age, experience, record, theoretical approach) with clients subjected to similar procedures and thereupon assessed on multiple measures of change: cognitive, affective and behavioural. Assessment devolves on rating scales, questionnaires and tests, with both short and long-term follow-ups. While this path runs the risk of opting for 'the incredibly difficult course over the relatively easy one' (Rowan, 1992: 162) multi-directional studies were begun and a good example is the Second Sheffield Psychotherapy Project (Shapiro et al. 1990). In this study researchers looked at differences between rival approaches, effects of variable treatment courses, comparisons between sample groups of clients and differences between individual therapists.

A preliminary paper issued by Sheffield Project came in for severe criticism from Paul Kline and it is worth summarising his views here in order to display the endless complexities with which such research must contend. He tells us that even the best studies have failed to overcome 'a depressing catalogue of problems' (Kline, 1992: 64) including such basic issues as the meaning of terms like 'recovery', 'presenting problem', 'therapy', controls for the effect of recent life events on the client and for the therapist's actual adherence to the theoretical model nominally employed. Still other problems concern the adequacy of sampling sizes, the validity of personality tests used in the initial assessment and the placebo problem inherent in assessing results. Moreover, as he points out, many of the questionnaire designs used to assess the helpfulness of the therapeutic session from the point of view of clients yield little more than the kind of subjective data which might be elicited from qualitative interviews or the therapy session itself.

To sum up so far: process research is unworkable due to the insoluble difficulties in using variable analysis to separate out what actually works in therapy, a problem that also applies to multi-directional research. Outcome research shows little evidence for the view that specific approaches are effective in general, or else reveals minimal differences between one type of psychotherapy and another. Even these claims depend on the assumption that therapists are actually following the procedures they were trained in; a view not confirmed by surveys. Meanwhile, authorities such as Arnold Lazarus tell us that what goes on in therapy works to an 'it depends' principle and a long line of researchers have failed to show in what way expert therapists differ from novices, nor whether therapists possess skills that can actually be taught. For example, Hattie (1984) reviewed 43 studies in which the effectiveness of professional therapists was compared to para-professionals (e.g. lecturers and teachers with a brief training in communication skills) and found that the latter group attracted better ratings than the former.

Meanwhile, Howarth (1989) tells us:

> One is driven to the simple conclusion that psychotherapists do not know what they are doing and cannot train others to do it, whatever it is.

Wilhelm Reich: the crux of the matter

Wilhelm Reich was responsible for some important revisions of psychoanalytic practice which later on became the foundation for other therapeutic schools, notably Reichian therapy, Gestalt therapy and Bioenergetic therapy. Reich suggested that many forms of neurosis were created by socio-economic conditions which distorted character formation in such a way that libido became blocked by rigid ego-resistances, thus inhibiting one's capacity for genitality and love; a view which, along with other delinquencies, led to his expulsion from the International Psychoanalytic Association in 1934. In contrast to the passive, non-committal, stance of the older analysts Reich insisted that therapy could only begin once the character resistances of the client had been actively identified and attacked. Since the client's character (or concretely, her communicative style) constituted the ego's defences against desire it was futile to begin the analysis until these had been broken down and the client made open to new material. In this Reich was at once both curiously 'Freudian' in an over-literal way and yet far removed from the general trend of Freud's influence.

As Charles Rycroft says:

> Reich's advocacy of character-analysis in addition or in preference to symptom-analysis and dream-interpretation also contributed to the realisation that the therapeutic effect of psychotherapy derives not from the unearthing of traumatic memories or from the correct interpretation of dreams but from the nature of the relationship between analyst and client. By insisting on the importance of analysing the client's defences against allowing spontaneous rapport to develop between himself and the analyst, he opened up the possibility of discovering what really goes on between them and

> contributed significantly to the idea that
> psychotherapy consists in a confrontation
> or encounter between two real, live,
> people. (Rycroft, 1971: 28-9)

In the mid-1920s Reich had been given a position of some responsibility in the Vienna Psychoanalytic Society. At Freud's command he had been made Director of the Technical Seminar, which met weekly to discuss clinical casework. It was thus directly concerned with psychotherapy and its problems rather than psychoanalytic theory. Reich's statements about analytic practice are interesting for the same reason as Lazarus's: both emerged from clinical experience in 'the trenches'.

In what follows Reich refers to a common clinical problem: what exactly should a therapist do with any given case and what rules are there to guide practitioners?

First Reich sets out the problem:

> It was only as long as there was little and
> unsystematic discussion of analytic
> technique that one could believe that
> analysts...had also developed a technique
> which was common to all...there was a

> wide divergence of opinion even with regard to everyday problems of analytic practice. If, for example, a certain resistance situation is presented...one analyst will say it calls for this measure, a second, another, and a third, still another. (Reich, 1950: 5-6).

Then he tells us that there must be 'one optimal technical procedure which in this situation is better than any other' (ibid.) before going on to tell us what it is:

> It took a long time before it became clear what is the crux of the matter: to derive the situation technique from each respective analytic situation itself by way of an exact analysis of its details. This method was strictly adhered to and proved highly valuable...Instead of giving advice, one discussed the difficulty, say a resistance situation, until the discussion itself spontaneously revealed the necessary measure; then one had the feeling that only that could be the right thing and nothing else. (ibid.)

These two passages, which defend Reich's departure from orthodoxy in pursuit of 'the optimal technical procedure', are replete with rhetorical arguments which create more problems than they solve. It is asserted that when therapists sit together to discuss case histories each calls for a different approach to the same client. However, the 'optimal' procedure is to take each clinical problem, situationally, as it comes. Which would surely result in the kind of disagreements which worried Reich to begin with. Noticeably, Reich begins with a tale about his weekly meetings with the Vienna Technical Seminar. To start in this way builds up a picture of confusion: psychoanalysts sitting around aimlessly disagreeing between themselves on basic principles of practice. The assertion that what little discussion about principles there had been, was 'unsystematic' leaves the way open for the more systematic discussion which follows. We will note also the contrasting, semi-live, spatial metaphors, in the English translation, of 'divergences' in (erroneous) opinions and the 'crux of the matter' which arrives at a correct view.

Subtly, Reich builds his warrants. We were told already that confusions in analytic techniques had arisen only so long as nobody had taken the trouble to hold a systematic discussion about them. Then we are told that 'a long time' had to elapse before 'it' became clear. The empirical 'it' which is then disclosed to the writer (and, perforce, to the reader) turns out to be the result of a yet more systematic investigation: the 'exact analysis' of the details of each analytic situation. 'It' is here being used as a floating indexical. While the context seems reasonably clear (the psychoanalytic session), the reference, at this stage, is far from being so. The implication is that the sentence to follow contains a revelatory truth. The fact that the revelation turns out to be a near tautology ('...to derive the situation technique....from each situation...') might easily be missed by its rhetorical positioning in the text as a statement in which a long anticipated disclosure is contained.

Taken altogether we have a closely designed yet extended empirical investigation which, in true scientific fashion, enters into matters which others have been too careless to address. The claim that the correct method, lacking in clinical detail as it is, was 'strictly adhered to' bolsters the air of experimental rigour, in which our investigator is not easily to be deterred from his pursuit of the optimal procedure. Despite the promise of empirically founded results derived from an investigation of cases (surely numerous?) which have occurred over a long time Reich's conclusion is, again, ambiguous:

> Our method is not a principle based on fixed procedures; it is a method which is based on certain basic theoretical principles but really determined by the individual case and the individual situation. (Reich, 1950: 6).

Psychotherapists hoping for the revelation of a 'technique common to all' and clinical tips on practice might be dismayed by a conclusion in which the new, correct, method is described first in terms of what it is not and then by way of an 'it depends' principle in which the therapeutic approach varies according to the client sitting opposite. We are told that the new method is not itself a principle but then that it is based on principles, a statement immediately qualified as to make even the latter assertion meaningless, for if the method is determined by the individual case it cannot rest on fixed principles but on the *in situ* judgement of the therapist. Which leads us back to Reich's starting point. Note, however, that the passage adroitly asserts an allegiance to psychoanalytic doctrines ('theoretical principles') while at the same time clearing a space for the analyst, in practice, to adopt whatever *ad hoc* procedures might be necessary to progress the treatment.

Reich's textual logic exemplifies the split between theory and practice: attempts to apply formalised procedures are unhinged by the demands of the therapeutic interview while the *in situ* practices actually used require rhetorical explanation if they are to be made to fit back into the theoretic claims made for them. Like Lazarus, his mode of practice is based on an 'it depends' argument. Therapy is accomplished by means of an interpretation of the client's presentations and by common-sense reasoning in which the therapist's responses are determined by a reading of the client's character and motivations, followed by the selection of a 'best fit' approach for the purposes in hand.

Tellingly, legitimation for Reich's practice proceeds by way of circularity. Reich defines psychotherapy (a method 'common to all') as, variously: analysis, discussion, procedure, technique, intuitive surmise and conversation. Tautologically, therapy is whatever is going on in the analytic hour (or, more precisely, whatever is represented at the Seminar as going on within the hour) and the sum of these activities make up the therapist's working methods. But when seeking to make therapeutic practice more rigorous and effective - thus fitting the criteria for therapy to be a science - the 'technique' is simply the name for what, in practice, are an indefinable set of intuitions.

2

PSYCHOTHERAPY AS DISCOURSE

THERAPY AND DISCOURSE - DISCOURSE ANALYSIS OF
THERAPEUTIC INTERVIEWS - LABOV AND FANSHEL -
THERAPY AS INDOCTRINATION: SZASZ AND GELLNER

---

*But before I treat a patient like yourself I need to
know a great deal more about him than the patient
himself can always tell me.*

T.S. Eliot, 1950. The Cocktail Party

Therapy and discourse

In the preceding chapter we raised some problems
in deciding what was to count as 'doing' psychotherapy: was it the theoretical method which therapists
claimed to be putting into practice, or was it the
improvisations that take place in any given session?
A look at the accounts provided by Lazarus and
Reich suggested an inconsistency on this issue
which each sought to resolve in different ways. Both

accounts suggested that psychotherapists are conversational opportunists who follow up promising turns in the conversation on an 'it depends' principle.

A second possibility is that that whenever therapists do therapy they participate in a therapeutic culture which is the real origin of their work. In this view they are participants rather than agents, actors rather than producers. On this view what we call psychotherapy is a type of discourse with elaborate rules to examine the self, confess faults and submit to a new set of rules for thinking, emoting and behaving. And therapy 'works' not because it is scientific but because it is a form of indoctrination.

One problem in using the term 'discourse' is that due to over-use it now has multiple meanings in different research contexts. As Potter & Wetherell (1987: 6-7) point out, it is possible to read works which purport to be about 'discourse analysis' which have little in common. One important reason for this outcome lies in the different working assumptions of those who describe what they do as discourse analysis. Thus the term has been variously used to refer to an analysis of cognitive processes, linguistic structures, conversational pragmatics and social action. In what follows the reader should bear in mind that I am not so much interested in discourse analysis but rather in investigating whether there is such a thing as 'therapeutic discourse' – a stylised way of thinking about, writing about, and doing therapy: "practices that systematically form the objects of which they speak" (Foucault, 1972: 49).

For Foucault, therapy is primarily a confessional practice (Foucault, 1981: 66-7), a 'ritual of discourse' (p61) linked to the injunction to examine the Self in order to know the truth about it and liberate oneself from it. But subjects, having scrutinised their actions in this way are drawn into the normalising practices of the social order; into a network of power relations (Fairclough, 1992: 53). It may be noticed that Foucault's idea of psychotherapy, as linked to the confessional act, is strongly influenced by psychoanalysis; a form of therapy which was much more common when he wrote his works on discourse than it is now. Even so, Foucault's survey is wide-ranging enough to allow for a view in which confessional discourses work as 'subjectifying' practices (ibid.) which bring personal affairs into the public arena in order to carry out a causal analysis, interpret the revelations given, codify them, and link them up to disciplinary routines in which deviance is corrected, information collated, and the individual himself is prescribed treatment. (Foucault, 1981: 65-67; Hutton, 1988).

There is a weakness in Foucault's abstract approach

which needs to be addressed here. It has much to do with Foucault's lack of interest in the concrete workings of discourse in everyday settings. Although his work, particularly that set out in *The Archaeology of Knowledge* was concerned with the general characteristics of discursive formations, not much attention is paid to actual examples of discourse-in-action. In general Foucault's interest lay in outlining the historical conditions of possibility for systems of thought not in the analysis of specific speech exchanges. This abstraction may be responsible for what some critics have seen as an exaggerated view of the power play of discourse (Macdonnell, 1986; Fairclough, 1992) and too little emphasis on its inconsistencies when put to work, the struggles between rival discourses, and (given the existence of conflicts) the opportunity to resist dominant discourses and play off one against another.

As Fairclough (1992: 46ff) also argues discourses are not fixed and they can evolve from their interaction with other discourses. For example, therapeutic discourse, and its concomitant interview practices, are continually being modified by the influence of medical, military, psychological, work-related, family and sexual discourses. Later on, as we shall note, transcripts from therapeutic interviews can provide evidence that clients, as well as therapists, are capable of deploying therapeutic

discourse in a variety of styles, for their own particular ends, or otherwise distancing themselves from
particular versions of discourse. For all these
reasons room needs to be made for a dialectical
view of therapy and the way in which therapeutic
discourse is open to change from above and below;
from social forces and from individual participation: in the home, the hospital, the training school,
the supervision room and from one interview to the
next and even on the telephone and in the casual
chit-chat which may begin and end the therapeutic
interview. Hence descriptions of therapeutic
discourse offered in this section stop short of
understanding it as fixed and domineering and,
instead, as interactive between the individual and
the social order.

Foucault's analysis influenced at least one influential
examination of psychotherapy as a social discipline:
Nikolas Rose's *Governing the Soul* (Rose, 1989). For
Rose, as for Foucault, therapeutic discourse is not
just used in the therapist's consulting room; in our
time it permeates our entire culture. It can be identified in schools and universities, hospitals and surg-
eries, on television and on the radio, in the office
and in the sitting room, in novels, magazines and
newspapers.

Here is a casual example from the agony column of
The Sun newspaper. In it the columnist gives advice

to a reader unable to choose between two lovers, one considerate and the other who mistreats her:

> *When we can't manage to do what every friend around us is urging on us for our own good, it is usually because there is a damaged bit of us that can't resist probing the old wound - a bit like you have to keep pressing an aching tooth to see if it really does still hurt. Micky takes you back to a feeling you've probably known since you were little. If you can't look after yourself by staying faithful to Freddy, get a counsellor's help to value yourself more highly. (The Sun, July 3rd 1997).*

Note that the 'wound' metaphor works together with an injunction to 'value' the self in a way that is recognisably therapeutic. Notice also the claim that failures to follow advice result from a 'damaged bit' of the self which requires the attention of a counsellor.

For Rose therapeutic discourse has its origins in ideology, in which a governing class seeks to mould individuals to become good citizens. In this perspective, therapeutic interviews are but one small means of transmitting this ideology and clients have already been introduced into its characteristic ways of thinking long before they reach the clinic. The history of psychotherapy, on this view, is symbiotic with social history.

As both Foucault (1981) and Ellenberger (1994) have shown, psychotherapy had a long history before Freud came on the scene. Its origins, first identifiable in institutional form from the end of the 18th century, were multiform. They included the confessional and 'the cure of souls', Renaissance dream-books, moral therapy, and mesmerism (Ellenberger, 1994: 43-246). As a word 'psychotherapy' seems to have been first used in 1889 (op. cit. p760) in connection with hypnotic modes of treatment before its pre-emption by Freud. It continued, however, to be used in connection with the rival approaches of hypnotherapy, Pierre Janet, van Renterghem and Paul Dubois up until the First World War. After that a psychiatric-psychoanalytic paradigm gets a purchase on the discipline until the emergence of new therapeutic schools in the 1950s.

Rieff, in an account which traces the historical roots of psychoanalysis and its successors, charts the rise of what he terms 'the therapeutic' ethic to the loss of a homogeneous social order in the industrialised West from the end of the nineteenth century onwards. Along with secularisation, the rise of individualism and a down-ranking of communal purposes, and the loss of stable social significations for the self and its actions, appeared a population of alienated individuals, ridden by anxiety and depression, who sought some way of reconciling the newly estranged self with the demands of the rising social order (Rieff, 1966).

On this view it follows that what therapists do is simply participate in discourses that bring their clients to them. They, like medical doctors, are not the originators of practices they implement. Their knowledge is the result of an accumulation of techniques, hypotheses, descriptions and procedures that are related back to other strategies of power within the social order. Indeed, taken to a rational extreme, this argument allows us to see therapeutic success as a kind of memory practice in which individuals are reoriented to their obligations as citizens. Certainly, the role of the therapist becomes fortuitous; it devolves upon the discursive practices through which her expertise is disseminated.

Foucault defined discourse as a 'ritual' in which participants re-enact knowledge-practices. While the existence of formulaic therapeutic forms is accepted some room must be made for personal agency if we are to coherently analyse how participants work to make therapy effective (or else fail to do so). Put another way, a comprehensive analysis looks at how these 'rituals' are worked up and utilised by participants and why (considered as a type of social interaction) they work so haphazardly within the therapy session. Any other course could not address the problem with which this work began: the apparent non-relationship between theory and practice in psychotherapy.

We will now look at psychotherapy at work in more detail and discuss whether or not it is possible to identify fixed rules of procedure ("knowledge practices") in therapeutic interviews. Throughout the discussion we will continue to refer to discourse as a social practice which uses talk and text to construct knowledge of various kinds but with a primary emphasis on how such discourses are employed and received in therapy.

Let us begin by looking at an experiment in social psychology (Garfinkel, 1967: 79-94) which deserves wider attention from psychotherapists. It reveals how, strictly speaking, one may not need the physical presence of a therapist in order to create the action of 'psychotherapy'. Ten undergraduates were induced into an experiment in which they understood they would be assisting in research into new counselling methods. In fact the real purpose of the study was to observe interpretative methods at work in making sense of an artificial therapeutic interview. Garfinkel was particularly interested in how participants employed a 'documentary method' in making sense of what was going on. Such a method takes the form of a hidden running commentary on the action which establishes an 'underlying pattern' to the interaction and relates emerging facts to the common-sense background knowledge held by the participant (op. cit. p78). Each student was assigned to an experimenter and told, falsely, that he was a counsellor-in-training. They were advised that, for the purposes of the study, the 'counsellor' was restricted to 'yes' or 'no' replies to their questions and would transmit his responses to them via an intercom from an adjacent room. In fact, prior to the interview, all the yes/no answers to come had been assigned randomly. The students were then asked to consult the counsellor on a significant personal issue.

Despite the sometimes 'senseless' answers received no student, as Garfinkel notes, was unable to complete the interview. All students were able to offer a convincing account for why the 'counsellor' replied as he did and in many cases accounts which explained incongruous answers attributed this either to the counsellor's ignorance of the facts, or alternatively to his superior wisdom, or to an unusual sensitivity to changing contextual factors as further questions and answers unfolded. The students (whose running commentaries on the interview were taped in between questions) performed a prodigious amount of hermeneutic work in order to fit the random 'yes' and 'no' interview answers to the problem posed. This work included doubts over their adequacies as question-setters, attributing hidden wisdom to the 'counsellor', the limitations of this way of doing therapy, and perceiving a narrative in which the counsellor was thought to be working towards an insight to be unravelled later on. Thus, their interpretative skills were brought to bear whenever a breach in the smooth flow of question and answer was perceived. It was noticeable how often the students would wait, in step-wise 'hopeful' fashion for sense to emerge from the answers by deferring judgement until later responses were received. Likewise, they were willing to revise their interpretations of prior answers in order to produce a fit with just-received answers. Still more interestingly it appears that the students were even willing to change their conception of what their problem was in order to maintain their sense that the advice received was relevant, truthful and consistent.

Taken together these routine devices for producing sense from random information are sophisticated and powerful enough to generate sufficient coherency for the interview to be understood by the recipient as 'therapeutic'. Garfinkel does not refer directly to the influence of 'therapeutic discourse' on the interpretative work carried out although examples are given of subjects deciding that answers were motivated by the counsellor's desire to 'help', to be 'objective' or to look for unseen psychological payoffs in the problem posed. For the purposes of the argument offered here it is sufficient to note that a recognisable type of psychotherapy can be carried through with minimal interventions from the therapist: the therapeutic setting is alone sufficient to trigger off a process of self-examination and potential change. This lends weight to the notion that therapeutic discourse works in a ritualistic way: the very act of turning up, confessing to a problem and examining oneself in relation to it, is enough to excite reflection and change.

The whole process is summarised by Heritage:

> The findings of the 'student counselling experiment' indicate that the subjects' pursuit of a consistent underlying pattern in the 'advice' they were receiving involved a scarcely conscious recourse to a vast and unpredictable range of considerations which, at best, had the status of partially formulated, recipe-like knowledge. These considerations were consulted in an apparently haphazard manner, being

> taken up, discounted and dropped 'as the
> situation demanded'. (Heritage, 1984: 93)

The student volunteers all knew what a counselling interview was and some even used this knowledge to explain how the unusual form of the interview was affecting the results obtained. Their ability to perform the work of confessing to a problem, and using 'yes' and 'no' answers to gather insight into their predicament, suggests that they are at least partly participating in a discursive practice. A coherent analysis of therapeutic interviews needs both to allow for the 'recipes' people bring to therapy and the creativity with which participants employ them.

Although we have defined discourse as linguistic practices that form the objects of which they speak, we should now make a further distinction. This lies between considering discourse as large-scale forms of knowledge, and discourse as social interaction. For example, the discourse of medicine brings into being rules of formation which govern the way that medical practitioners talk and write about bodies, pathology, surgery, pharmacology, health, etc. A discourse analysis which looked at operations on this level of abstraction would differ from an analysis which examined a transcript of one particular medical interview. In the same way, a comprehensive view of what is going on in psychotherapy would need to consider both therapeutic discourses and specific interactions between therapists and clients. Considering psychotherapy as a discipline, the fact that it takes place through interviews is one of its most salient characteristics. The question then arises: does the interview setting, in which an acknowledged expert is priming a client recreate discourse? Are therapeutic interviews marked by speech characteristics peculiar to therapy?

One starting point is to look at interactional controls in therapy, such as the regulation of turns, which decide who is to speak at any given point. In one study of therapeutic interviews comprising 48 hours of talk one researcher noted that it was typically the therapist who initiated the business of therapy and who regulated closure of the interview (Ferrara, 1994: 43). Once the invitation to talk is issued the client may hold the floor for some time in order to state a problem or review events since the last meeting. Fairclough (1992: 54) links this feature of therapeutic work to confessional practices. While the client is in confessional mode the therapist tends to restrict her talk to non-lexicals (e.g. 'mm-hmm' and 'oh!') which keep the narrative going. This leads to some asymmetry in turn-taking in the opening part of the interview and, according to

Winefield et. al. (1987), over the first few interviews
in general. They coded tapes relating to approximately 90 interview hours, and concluded that the
course of therapy is marked by increasing
symmetry as the work progresses. That is, the
client's speech-count tends to diminish as that of the
therapist rises. However, the argument for asymmetry is not backed up by other research although,
in fairness, the amount of published material
containing content analyses of therapeutic interviews is paltry. It could also be that the view that
psychotherapy is driven in the first place by a
confessional has become a convention. It may also
be due to the fact that the psychodynamic and
person-centred counselling approaches which were
amongst those most studied in the 1970s and 1980s
are both non-directive styles that seek to elicit
narratives from the client. It may be, therefore, that
asymmetry is more noticeable if these approaches
are the subject of research and would appear less, if
not at all, in other approaches. This is especially
true for directive styles such as Cognitive-Behaviour
Therapy.

In a half-hour interview between Fritz Perls (Gestalt
therapy) and one client (Shostrom, 1966 - see below,
Chapter 4) approximately 58% of the talk was
taken up by the client - a rather slight imbalance. In
another, slightly shorter, interview by Albert Ellis

(Rational-Emotive Behaviour therapy) with the same client the proportion of talk taken up by the client was just 35%. Both were first interviews. If these examples are anything to go by then it must seem that asymmetry is either a feature restricted just to therapy of a certain type, or that symmetry varies widely from one interview to another.

Ferrara holds that therapeutic discourse is characterised by different kinds of 'repetition' (1994: 5). She classifies two main types of repetition in therapy: echoing (client repeats back a portion of, or all of, the therapist's utterance), and mirroring (therapist partially repeats client's utterance). Echoing, she claims, is used to signal 'emphatic agreement' on issues best known to the client (p113) while mirroring is associated with 'an indirect request for an expansion of what has just been said (p119). Both are linked to what she considers the 'essence' of psychotherapy: the pursuit of 'insight or self-understanding' (p108). The idea is that repetition works either to confirm the accuracy of self-examinations or to encourage more of the same. However, as Ferrara herself remarks (p124), repetition is used extensively in ordinary conversations as well as in the law courts, in police procedures, and other consultative genres. It is therefore hard to argue that there is anything distinctive about its use in therapy unless one has already made up one's mind that therapy is equivalent to the search for self-understanding (rather than change) and that mirroring and echoing are the means for achieving it.

Similar objections can be raised to the other features she puts forward as distinctive in therapeutic discourse: narrative retelling, collaborative metaphor and aligned turn-taking (in which therapists and clients assist each other in finishing sentences). Ferrara describes her book as 'complementary' to Labov and Fanshel's work on therapeutic discourse. As such it is subject to exactly the same objections which I will apply to that work shortly.

Winefield, Chandler and Bassett (1989) claim that tag questions featured heavily in their analysis of one client's contributions to a course of psychoanalytic therapy and argue that her increasing use of them correlate to increasing power and decreasing dependency on the therapist. Tag questions are interrogative forms added on to utterances (e.g. 'isn't it?', 'doesn't it?') and opinion differs widely concerning their function in speech. Levinson (1983: 365) asserts that tag-questions act as turn-taking regulators which would be consistent with the client handing the floor over to her therapist more often as therapy progressed successfully (in which case this would demonstrate increasing dependency on the therapist rather than the reverse).

Other candidates for the status of a 'recipe' for psychotherapy include metaphor and formulation. Therapeutic metaphors will be considered later on in this book in some detail, as will formulations, and I will come to a discussion of these topics in their proper place. However, in neither case can it be shown that they can be made to work without extensive, and context-sensitive, interpersonal negotiation between therapists and clients.

Labov and Fanshel: 'incoherent therapy'

Labov and Fanshel's (1977) work on therapeutic discourse would require attention in these pages in any event since no discussion of the subject would be complete without reference to this influential work. Conveniently, since it contains a view of therapy which is directly opposed to the conversational perspective I am (gradually) working towards here it can be utilised by way of contrast.

Labov and Fanshel's book offers an intensive analysis of a fifteen-minute segment of one interview with a 19-year old anorexic client in New York in the 1960s. In their book therapeutic discourse is identified as a speech-exchange in which one person seeks the help of another, who is an acknowledged expert in the resolution of psychological distress. Therapeutic interactions, for them, are marked by 'stigma' since the client, in coming for therapy, is 'socially defined as...not fully able to take care of himself' (p32). This gives rise, they claim, to an asymmetry of roles for the therapist is classed as more socially competent than the client. The purpose of therapy is for the client to get well but this must be achieved without offering help for, if assistance were offered, she would merely be confirmed in her helplessness. Therapists seek to solve this asymmetry - the imbalance in social competence - by not giving direct advice:

> The distinctive 'character of the therapeutic interview is that this help will be given only through further talk. (p31)

For Labov and Fanshel the therapist's role is a 'passive' reflecting one (p32) and I note, in passing, that the type of psychotherapy they analysed was of the psychodynamic counselling type. Despite this minimalist role they can expect to encounter resistance as clients seek to demonstrate that they are no longer in need of therapeutic attention.

Having established their arbitrary definition of

psychotherapy their book goes on to identify a machinery for analysis in which speech-acts used by participants are identified and linked to the social actions implied in them (p74-76). For example, speech-acts might call for the client to exert care for the self, repeat a request for information, or challenge the client's version of events. Or reciprocally, the client might deny that care is required, avoid offering more information or challenge the therapist's version of events. So long as these actions can be identified therapists and clients are deemed to be participating in therapy. Where no speech-acts can be identified discourse is deemed to be 'incoherent'. In the introduction to their work, Labov and Fanshel give an example of what they see as gibberish from a psychiatric interview with a young patient which shows up the flaws in their own approach.

Dr. What is your name?

Client: Well, let's say you might have thought you had something from before, but you haven't got it any more.

Dr. I'm going to call you Dean.

(cited in: Labov & Fanshel, 1977: 2)

While Labov & Fanshel assert that this exchange is nonsensical it does not take much ingenuity to read Dean as indeed carrying out a speech act which has an underlying coherence: in this case an indirect refusal to give his name by a play on the convention in psychiatric interviews in which the interviewer asks for information he already has. Curiously, this seems to fit their own definition of therapeutic discourse quite well. But because they do not consider Dean's position in this interview the deeper meaning of his answer escapes them. Indeed, Dean's words could be read as an exceptionally witty play on the psychiatrist's opening question. The imperative 'let's say' alerts us that something is being done with speech which is not what it seems; the 'might have' clause to the fact that the psychiatrist is pretending not to know Dean's name; and the rest of the answer is a double play on the knowledge which the psychiatrist claims not to have and to the disappearing relationship he might once have had with his client. It is important to note, too, that Dean's 'ill-formed' reply effectively re-casts the social identity of his interlocutor. The psychiatrist's question implies a listener who is mentally defective. Dean's reply, by contrast, presupposes a respondent who never listens because he is never there: he is instead the voice of an anonymous and alienating institution. It is this very absence which Dean addresses in the despair marked by an allusive play on words which is no longer limited by the attentions of someone who might be seriously interested in what he has to say.

The distinction drawn here lies between well-formed discourse and ill-formed. That, as we have seen, is the subject of Labov and Fanshel's dissertation: the presentation of a set of rules of discourse which enable the analysis of a therapeutic conversation to proceed and so to display the rule-governed nature of such conversations (Labov & Fanshel, 1977: 3-4). If speech can be analysed in terms of the therapeutic action performed by the speaker in response to the previous utterance, or to the context of therapy, then it is well-formed and its analysis as therapeutic discourse becomes possible. If no speech-acts can be identified then it is ill-formed and can be relegated to the status of incoherent raving. But it might be argued: how can we decide in advance whether discourse is ill-formed or not unless we have some idea of the context in which speakers are working; the subject positions they have adopted; and the way in which they are mutually attending to what either has to say?

Although Labov & Fanshel draw attention to the asymmetry of roles between therapist and client their awareness of this point does not impact on their analysis of the talk which they read as an unproblematic index of speech acts and external facts. For example, they persist in treating the client's narrative of her family problems as a (disguised) account of her failure to do therapy without once considering the strategic role it plays in being told to that therapist, in that way, and at that time. Only by ignoring the argumentative quality of the client's talk can Labov and Fanshel continue with their project. It is worth noting here that while Labov and Fanshel availed themselves of the therapist's commentary on the interview they did not do so for Rhoda (the client). Yet it is precisely Rhoda's contributions which produce the therapeutic material they analyse.

The opening section of the Labov & Fanshel's transcript is reproduced below (R = Rhoda. T = Therapist):

1 R.: I don't know whether ... I - I think I did the right thing, jistalittle situation came up an' I tried to uhm well, try to use what I - what I've learned here, see if it worked

2 Th.: Mhm

3 R.: Now, I don't know if I did the right thing. Sunday um my mother went to my sister's again.

4 Th.: Mm-hm

5 R.: And she usu'lly goes for about a day or so, like

if she leaves on Sunday, she'll come back Tuesday morning

6 Th.: Hm

7 R.: So - it's nothing. But she lef' Sunday, and she's still not home.

8 Th.: O - oh

9 R.: And ... I'm getting a little nuts a'ready. I's ... I haven't been doin' too much school work because - here this has to be done, here that has to be done, an...I really - I'm getting tired. It - it's I have too much to do, an' I can' con'trate on any one thing.

10 Th.: Mhm

11 R.: So ... it's in - it's not that I - ... I mean I - I've proved, I know that I can get along without my mother, it isn't that - I - I - can't get along without her but it - I know that when I don't have any school, an' she's gone way - she went away for a week, an' a half an' it didn't bother me in the leas'.

12 Th.: Mhm

13 R.: But it seems that - I have jist - a little too much t'do. So at first, I wasn' going to say anything. Then I remembered - that - if I keep it in what's bothering me -

14 Th.: Mhm

15 R.: then nobody knows an' everybody thinks everything is fine, and good

16 T.: Mhm

17 R.: and I end up - hurting my self.

18 Th.: Right

19 R.: Which would be that if I kept letting her stay there and didn' say 'Look - uh - I mean y'been there long enough.' I'd jus' get tired, an-nd I I'm not doing my school work right.

20 Th.: Mhm

21 R.: An-nd so - when - I called her t'day, I said, 'Well, when do you plan to come home? So she said, 'Oh, why?' An-nd I said, 'Well things are getting just a little too much! [laugh] This is - i's jis' getting too hard, and and ...... I - She s'd t'me, Well, why don't you tell Phyllis that?' So I said, 'Well, I haven't talked to her lately.' And - uh ... I'm just gonna tell her. Now ..... I think I did the right thing, I think that -

22 Th.: Yes, I think you did, too. Well, what's your question? You know, you have a lot of guilt about it, you have a very full schedule at school.

23 R.: Yes, it's a little -

24 Th.: Now what about Aunt Editha, she doesn't help you in the house?

(Labov & Fanshel, 1977: 363-364. Transcript layout modified).

Labov & Fanshel characterise the segment as an example of the client's resistance to therapy followed by the therapist's attempt to have her acquire more autonomy, express her feelings and gather some self-insight. They tell us that Rhoda starts the session by asserting that she has in fact carried out the thera-peutic proposition that she should express her wishes to other family members and that she continues with a narrative representation of her independent status, which story (they say) fails to support her claim. In their version the narrative demonstrates that she cannot cope with her mother's absence and cannot fulfil her household role obligations. She challenges her mother's non-fulfilment of these duties with an indirect request for her to come home but thereby displays her inability to support herself. Rhoda ends with a coda in which she reasserts her claims to be putting therapeutic propositions into practice but is interrupted by the therapist. The therapist expresses exasperation (Labov and Fanshel provide us with a graph of her voice pitch), queries Rhoda's uncer-tainty on the issue and draws attention to her guilt in expressing her needs to mother. She challenges

Rhoda to examine her own emotions on these issues with the aim of indirectly forcing her to gain insight into her maladjustment.

I now offer a reading in which this segment could be understood as an ironic narrative. An ironic narrative is one amongst three defined by Gergen and Gergen (1986; 1987) to describe the different genres into which a narrative might fall. Thus a tragic narrative relates a tale of a regress from good fortune to bad, while a comic story tells of progress from a dismal state of affairs to a better. An ironic narrative, by contrast, relates no progress at all. It is a genre which displays stagnation where progress might have been expected. Examples include Charles Dickens' *Great Expectations* and Kurt Vonnegut's *Breakfast of Champions*. In both novels there is a rejection of the view that individual or social changes imply progress, whatever appearances might suggest to the contrary.

In this reading the position reallocated to Rhoda would be one similar to Dean's - that of an ironical commentator on therapeutic conventions. To make this reading work requires only that we apply a new footing arrangement to the transcript as read. Briefly, 'a footing' refers to the position speakers have taken up in relation to their own assertions (Antaki, 1994: 129). That is, in order to make sense of the accounts offered listeners and analysts have to decide on the relationship adopted by the speaker in relation to what they have to say. For example, a therapist might relate an anecdote concerning the successful outcome of one case to a client with the aim of providing some clues concerning the way in which the client himself might make progress. Clearly, if we read the story as if the therapist were the principal (that is, as if it summarised her own position) it would carry a very different meaning from a reading in which she was the animator (the transmitter of the story). While the former case might entail a reading of the story as a straightfor-ward tutorial the latter invites the hearer to apply it to her own case. Where Labov and Fanshel persist in reading Rhoda's talk as if it were offered by the client-as-principal I argue that it is just as plausible to read it as coming from the animator position. In which Rhoda intends her therapist to understand her words not as a story about herself but as a commentary on the failure of therapy so far.

Rhoda's narrative is more or less continuous from lines 1-21 and conveys an 'if it weren't for them' story-line in which her college work is being held up due to the lack of help available around the house. With only one exception (line 22) the therapist's contributions are restricted to non-lexical prompts ('Mhm') which allow the narrative to proceed. Such narratives of everyday life, we are told (p104-105) are frequently employed as representations of past experience which carry an underlying proposition. The task of interpretation, then, centres on the proposition conveyed by the tale we have. For Labov & Fanshel the story is intended to back up the claim that the client is trying hard to put the lessons of therapy into practice in expressing her needs to other family members. It is a representation which 'mitigates' Rhoda's true predicament and 'masks' her resistance to therapy. However, we are not told of the way in which they have matched this narrative to a set of externally available facts since, as they say, all the 'facts' are provided by Rhoda in her narrative. Indeed, the very presentation of this story as a factual one by Rhoda is itself significant in opening up the exchange to other readings.

It is important to note that the narrative is produced by Rhoda and is also about Rhoda. In this version we are provided with an account in which the subject-of-psychotherapy relates a story in which the subject of the tale attempts to put into practice some therapeutic lessons ('if I keep it in what's bothering me...then I end up hurting myself.'). The story seeks to exonerate her from the charge that her problems are of her own making. This much can be read from line 7 in which it means 'nothing' for Mother to be away, and line 11 in which Rhoda disallows the alternative explanation for the troubles related in the narrative: that she is too anorexic to remain independent for long. By externalising her predicament in this way Rhoda gradually puts together a set of reasons why therapy cannot succeed. It is striking that the narrative is punctuated by a succession of problems created by other people: the non-arrival of mother at line 7, the sense of going 'nuts' and getting 'tired' at line 9, things 'bothering' her (line 13) and getting 'too much' and 'too hard' in line 21. This is the 25th session and, if this a record of therapeutic progress, it reads like a very strange one. As an ironic narrative, however, it succeeds perfectly.

What could this version of events which contains an agent who is not the narrator, nor either the client who does not succeed in carrying out therapeutic advice, be designed to do? It performs the conventional function of delivering material for the ears of the therapist but, more importantly, it takes the client out of the arena of psychotherapy in the same way that Dean makes himself impervious to the psychiatrist's question. But her therapist, like Dean's psychiatrist, does not display any recognition of the shifting identities before her. Like Labov & Fanshel (or perhaps because of them) her replies are reported as limited to what she hears as the 'facts' of the case: Rhoda has failed to carry out instructions just as Dean has failed to give his name. Dean &

Rhoda's positions are interchangeable in that it is Rhoda who elects not to reveal her identity and Dean who decides not to follow instructions.

The problem with Labov & Fanshel's analysis is that it treats psychotherapy as a pre-constituted object such that any speech-exchange between therapists and clients can be elaborated upon as a canonical example of it. This is to make a category-mistake in which 'examples' of therapeutic talk are held to refer to some ghostly entity which stands behind it and is nominalised as 'psychotherapy'. An artificial and restricted view of therapy as a matter of covert persuaders struggling with clients who want to evade responsibility and shake off the social stigma of doing therapy is not one that most therapists would recognise. One can only be amazed that they both spent nine years analysing one 15-minute segment from one therapy session and concluded that this small excerpt represented every other therapy session that had ever been held.

Szasz & Gellner: Therapy as indoctrination

We now turn to another interpretation of therapeutic discourse which is also an ideological critique - the claim that therapy is an indoctrination process in which participants are duped into a knowledge-practice administered by a guild of cult members.

Gellner's idea of psychotherapy is that is a process in which entrants are introduced into an enclosed belief system administered by self-appointed experts who have received a prior indoctrination into the method proffered (Gellner,1992; 1993). While he reserves most of his fire for psychoanalysis in particular his arguments may fairly be extended to what he calls "Freud-and-water counsellors" (Gellner, 1992: 63).

Briefly, Gellner defines psychotherapy as a form of 'mysticism', which he describes as:

> ...an intense emotional experience, which purports to be and is felt as being the acquisition of knowledge and which is important, privileged and out of the ordinary. (Gellner, 1992: 41).

Such experiences result in intense feelings for the therapist which accident thereby 'appears to confirm the validity both of the theoretical and the specific insights attained in the course of the therapeutic sessions...' (Gellner, 1992: 51-52). This mystical experience arises from a setting in which there is a suspension of everyday beliefs expressed in 'objective language' and, jettisoning these, a willing submission to an 'addictive' ideology espoused by a member of a 'charismatic community' of believers, who have themselves been initiated into the order (Gellner, 1993: 45-55). Clients then undergo a re-evaluation of their motives and identity in terms of an interpretative code which is itself backed up by a set of culturally received ideas about human nature: its hidden instinctual hunger, infantile greed, sexual promiscuity, distorted perceptions and animistic fears (op. cit. p11ff). Such ideas are often embedded, within the theory, by 'simple-minded physical metaphor[s]' (Gellner, 1992: 52) which encapsulate psychic processes. Examples include a hydraulic mechanism of energy; a 'homunculus' metaphor of the inner self; and that of the 'transference' (Gellner, 1993: 95).

Psychotherapy is thus a persuasive experience and matters go awry only insofar as practitioners attempt to marry their semi-mystical incantations with scientific truth. Claims to scientific validity are misleading since their results are strictly due to the emotional effects felt after a *rite de passage* into what Gellner sees as a pseudo-religion (p41-42). It is a faith which derives its attractiveness from its ability to overcome the failure to accommodate the demands of the instincts within an alienating and 'disenchanting' twentieth century social order (p213-214).

Even so, there are more sinister influences at work:

> Not only are clients provided with a linguistic explanatory framework that 'makes sense" of their experiences, but the power relations within the analytic setting and beyond that in the institutions of psychoanalysis (with their right of expulsion and excommunication of those who subvert their values) enforce its adherence. The training analysis, rite of initiation into the body of the movement, ensures the perpetuation of the values and words of the high priests of analytic doctrine...In being hidden and denied but also immensely powerful and domineering, the demand for commitment made by psychoanalysis can drift near to exploitation. (p225-226)

Gellner claims that psychotherapy is an 'intense emotional experience' which is somehow false. It 'purports' to be a form of knowledge and 'appears' to be valid. Presumably, then, it is not either of these. It is, for Gellner, a misleading gloss on the real nature of the client's experience. But what is functioning as the truth here? The first thing to notice is

that Gellner's account rests on his claims to knowledge concerning the experience of therapy. But no
empirical analysis is supplied by him in either of the
accounts cited. Even if there were it is by no means
certain that therapeutic talk of any kind could
demonstrate its own untruth. For Gellner's account
to work there must be a resort to another order of
reality which explains the processes of
psychotherapy better than therapists and clients can
themselves. This, in turn, must be able to tell us
what psychotherapy 'really' is - a kind of false
consciousness which masks the truth. Broadly, Gellner's argument rests on the claim that psychotherapy
lacks 'horizontal' connections with facts and events
that take place outside therapy (Gellner, 1992: 48).
He complains that the truth of therapy is only ever
validated by its participants, not with reference to
other domains of knowledge. To overcome this he
calls for the procedures of therapy to be 'operationalised' in that there should be 'impersonal' rules
for determining what any given term means within
the therapeutic interview (op. cit. p47). But, as we
have seen, only interactants can decide on the
meaning and direction of the terms they employ in
therapeutic conversations. To assume otherwise is, in
itself, an arbitrary construction on what is going on
in therapy. In this respect Gellner's assertions mirror
the therapeutic practices he so dislikes. He, as thera-

pists sometimes do, offers an 'explanatory framework' which 'makes sense' of the matter under discussion. Power relations, invested in the academic institution to which he belongs (the University of Cambridge), play their part in securing 'adherence' for his views. Meanwhile, the 'values and words' of sociological analysis no doubt require 'initiation' if they are to influence the reader. As such we can view Gellner's critique as a conflict between two different types of power or, more simply, as a reflection of Gellner's distaste for therapeutic vocabularies and his preference for sociological ones.

Szasz also argues that psychotherapy is a covert means of persuasion which works by re-writing the client's problems. This move relies on a 'double language' in which terms used by clients are switched into a lexicon of terms used by the therapist (see also Gellner, 1993: 189ff). On this view individuals suffering from a variety of common-sense 'problems in living' (Szasz, 1972) arrive for cures and their difficulties are translated into the jargon of psychotherapy.

Like Gellner, Szasz argues that the therapists rely on dominance rather than on practices which produce new knowledge. Relying, as they do, on coercion or on 'hidden' exploitation therapists cannot, necessarily, produce anything more than metaphors or myths which are a misleading gloss on the client's predicament.

For Szasz, '...psychotherapeutic interventions are metaphorical treatments' (Szasz, 1978: 5). They too, it appears, are rituals in which clients' concrete distress is glossed in terms of therapeutic vocabularies employed by those they consult. In this way therapy is '....the name we give to a particular kind of personal influence....' (Szasz, 1978: 9).

In an earlier work he locates this personal influence in a translation of the client's words into the code of psychotherapy:

> The transformation...of presentational symbols into conventional signs...such as occurs in the course of psychoanalysis and some forms of psychotherapy, must thus be seen as itself constituting a process of personality change. (Szasz, 1972: 131-132).

Here 'presentational symbols' refer to expressions of distress, covert requests for help, and narratives about the problem (see Szasz, 1972: 128-131). 'Conventional signs', by contrast, are contained in discourses which have abstract, general references which rest on arbitrary denotations (Szasz, 1972:

112). Szasz has mostly in mind interpretations in which the client's issues are recast into the jargon of psychoanalysis but his point holds good for other types of therapy.

Such a transformation is, in Szasz's terms, metaphorical, assuming metaphor to be a transformation of information from one code into another. Psychoanalysis and its derivatives, according to Szasz, are complete systems of re-inscription which reify the concrete communications of the client into the outward symptoms of formally treatable disorders - which symptoms happen to be the very ones which are identified and explained in the therapist's lexicon. This is the 'myth' in which the client comes to acquiesce as a means of relieving their distress.

There is an anti-ideological thrust to Szasz's arguments which should be acknowledged if we are to make his critique intelligible. Like Gellner and Rose he sees therapy in terms of dominance and mystification. As we have seen, his argument is similar to Gellner's in that he claims that therapy works discursively by applying a double register to the language of the client and that the client is persuaded in the rites of therapy. But he parts company with Gellner in his further claim that psychotherapy (which in his book *Ideology and Insanity* he seems to consider as interchangeable with psychiatry) is an ideology of mental health which oversees 'the conversion of ideas into social levers' of power (1973: 68).

On this reading psychotherapists are colluding in an oppressive ideology insofar as they set themselves out to treat deviants with a 'mental illness' although it should be added that Szasz does make room for a 'libertarian' form of therapy which works with individuals to resolve their concrete problems in living. Separated from the disciplines of natural science, pharmacology and medicine the work of such a libertarian therapist would be to act solely in the interests of the client and work to the directions set by him, not the state. She would retain an awareness of 'politics and ethics' and their potential influence on the client's predicament, the better to be able to offer well-formed advice (op. cit. p228ff). Finally, she would be guided by an approach in which the clients' words are taken as an accurate guide to their predicament not as a mask for psychopathology. This model of therapy is consistent with the one offered later in this book. However, as I will argue, it requires more than a simple resort to 'concrete discourse' and the rejection of metaphors to make it work. In the next chapter I examine the use of metaphor in psychotherapy and will try to show that metaphors, when they work at all, can only do so with the implicit co-operation of the client.

3

PSYCHOTHERAPY AND METAPHOR

A good metaphor is something even the police should keep an eye on.

Lichtenberg. Aphorism 98

One way of summarising the Szasz-Gellner critique of psychotherapy is that it claims that clients are enrolled into a knowledge-practice in which a set of key ideas and theories expressed through dominant metaphors are imposed, covertly, on the subject. Although this objection to the abuse of power is not denied I argue that it over-simplifies things by assuming that psychotherapy is a disguised mono-logue. A close examination of interview work suggests that clients are as much originators of, or

participants in, therapeutic discourse as are therapists. An examination of how metaphors work is a
test case.

Many therapists, it would seem, acquiesce in the
view that metaphor is fundamental to
psychotherapy although, naturally, most see this
feature as benign rather than sinister. Thus
metaphor has been claimed to play a role, within
therapy, in promoting self-initiated learning in the
client (Coombs & Freedman, 1990); the transmis-
sion of moral & cultural information (Gordon,
1978); in self-discovery (Hobson, 1985; Angus,
1992); as a form of indirect communication which
facilitates personal change (Haley, 1976); and the
recovery of repressed memories (Giannitrapain,
1987). As Jay Haley, an American psychotherapist
and researcher with over forty years experience in
the field puts it '...the use of analogies, or
metaphors, seems especially central to the procedures of therapy.' (Haley, 1976: 85)

For Gregory Bateson (a colleague of Haley's) a
'metaphor compares things without spelling out the
comparison.' (Bateson, 1972: 56). In this comparison view of metaphor two previously unrelated
items, one 'the vehicle' and the other the 'focus' are
brought together in such a way that the focus takes
on a different meaning. For example, in the
metaphor 'men are grass' the focus term 'men' is

likened to a vehicle - 'grass' - that grows for a season and then dies, to be replaced by fresh grass.

On this view psychotherapy re-schematises the client's ideas (the focus) in terms of an 'explanatory framework' (the vehicle) providing a substitute set of cognitive filters through which the world can be perceived anew. It implies that there is something sneaky about this as the basis for comparison is kept hidden from the client who in turn fails to recognise the ritual to which he has been introduced. In other, more favourable views, the therapist simply deploys the universal use of metaphor to therapeutic ends:

....metaphor is an indispensable tool of thought and expression - a characteristic of all human communications, even that of the scientist. (Bateson, 1972: 205).

Psychotherapy, as characterised by Bateson (1972: 190-193), is a relearning process which seeks, through metaphor, to excite changes in the client's ideas. Psychotherapists communicate new ideas to clients in a way which is emotionally and intellectually evocative of change, not with any intention to manipulate but to invite exploration and promote a re-synthesis of thought, memory and emotion

(Hobson, 1985). Given that clients as well as thera-pists will inevitably communicate in metaphor, psychotherapy, rather than being manipulative, is just a little more openly metaphorical in orientation than other types of exchange.

I want to argue that both the pejorative and the appreciative versions of therapeutic metaphor are, if not mistaken, then at least incomplete. Since both views depend on the assumption that metaphor gets to work principally on the internal cognitions of the client then their claims can only hold good so long as metaphor is understood as a carrier of ideas from one domain to another. These claims also rely on the assumption that the message will always reach its destination, a supposition certainly not borne out in clinical practice, as some researchers have noted. For example, Angus looked into the function of specific metaphors in therapeutic inter-views and found that conclusions concerning their actual impact were, at best, tentative:

>...we still know very little about how individual metaphor phrases come to symbolise shared contexts of meaning over the course of a complete therapy. (Angus, 1992: 207).

One difficulty is that the way in which hearers work out that something is a metaphor can be hard to track. Some metaphors are dead, some live, some half-dead, while others are indistinguishable from jokes, puns and slips of the tongue. A related difficulty concerns identification: some tropes (particularly irony) would be very difficult to identify without an exhaustive examination of the conversational context, even the paralinguistic cues, which accompany them. A third problem lies in the problem of changing context and the related difficulty of identifying metaphoric usages within those episodes: a literal phrase elicited from one interview may represent a conceit which refers to something said on another occasion; some subtle, metonymic chains may be worked up in the conversation over the whole therapeutic hour while quite striking analogies might be developed in just a few words. A final difficulty is that, supposing we are able to identify a portion of speech as a metaphor, we cannot be sure that such speech is being treated metaphorically by the listener in the way intended by the speaker. As Angus again warns:

> It is striking how often therapists and clients have distinctly different private imaginal representations of the same

> metaphor spoken in a session. (Angus,
> 1992: 208).

Note that this difficulty in tracing the operation of therapeutic metaphor arises precisely in relation to claims that metaphors act to change cognitions. Since there is no guarantee that the metaphors do, in fact, work in this way, their use is always open to the possibility that they will be misheard, unappreciated, discarded or re-interpreted in unforeseen directions.

I want now to offer a counter-argument to the comparison view of metaphor borrowed from an influential essay on metaphor by Davidson (1978) and to extend it into the arena of psychotherapy.

In Davidson's non-comparison view, 'metaphors mean what the words, in their most literal interpretation, mean, and nothing more.' (Davidson, 1978: 30). Although this may sound paradoxical and intentionally provocative it draws attention to the way in which metaphors work by implication rather than semantics and require creative work if they are to be brought off. Metaphor is a matter of linguistic usage rather than semantic meaning (op. cit. p31); like lies, hints and promises the original purpose of the metaphor is secondary to the way it is taken up by the recipient (p41). Appeals to the literal meaning conveyed by metaphor are both unarguable and unnecessary. Unarguable because claims that metaphors alter thoughts cannot explain why anyone should want to use metaphor for this purpose when plain prose would do (ibid.) and unnecessary because a pragmatic account is alone adequate for the purposes of explaining its conversational function. All that is required is to allocate rather more credit to interpreters than the comparison view allows:

> Metaphor is the dreamwork of language and, like all dreamwork, its interpretation reflects as much on the interpreter as on the originator. The interpretation of dreams requires collaboration between a dreamer and a waker, even if they be the same person; and the act of interpretation is itself a work of the imagination. So too understanding a metaphor is as much a creative endeavour as making a metaphor, and as little guided by rules. (p29).

Since metaphors are not (obviously) true in a literal sense (e.g. 'man is a wolf') then they signal that the hearer is to search for some state of affairs in which they could become true (e.g. people sometimes act like pack-animals). In that way metaphors act as an 'extension of discourse' (Soyland, 1994) and belong 'exclusively to the domain of use' (Davidson, 1978: 31) rather than meaning. The literal sense of the words used are taken up in such a way that that new applications are sought for them other than those established by linguistic usage. In his wide-ranging discussion of metaphor Cooper concludes that users of metaphor can only employ them on the implicit assumption that listeners will be able to identify it as a metaphor:

> The intention to speak metaphorically, and the recognition of this intention by others, cannot be an inessential feature of metaphorical talk. (Cooper, 1986: 278).

Naturally, what is to count as an instance of a 'literal' statement and what is to count as 'metaphor' within a particular conversation will be for interlocutors to decide and the distinction may only be observable for analysts from noticing the way in which either party treats the utterance.

If it is not true that metaphors signal that the utterance is to be taken non-literally then everything said would be an actual or potential metaphor and we would be unable to treat fact and fancy in different ways. Since, as we have seen it is the paradoxical, apparently nonsensical character of metaphor, taken literally, which signals that the hearer is being primed for some extra interpretative work, then novel uses of language will always take place against the mutually accepted, common-sense, background of literal facts and propositions. The contrast between established use and potentially new, poetic use, typically affords the recognition that the speaker is using a simile, an analogy, or irony, hyperbole, synecdoche, etc. to make a non-factual point. No trope could fire without this contrast with the literal. Even in psychotherapy, therefore, metaphors could not work at all without an at least implicit reliance on the client's ability to recognise and use metaphor. This leads to the further conclusion that metaphors cannot work in an underhand way: there must be some form of collaboration between interlocutors concerning its successful introduction into the exchange.

Consider the following example of a therapeutic interaction involving metaphor. The excerpt is taken from the second interview between a therapist and a 37 year old married male client complaining of relationship difficulties. In it the reader will find an example of talk in which the introduction of metaphor misfires. Dream material offered by the client is treated metaphorically and its usage extended. But this gambit does not succeed within this particular interview as the client cannot find a use for the metaphor. The extract begins just after the client has related a dream in which he was trapped on a fairground ride while being observed by a lion watching from the shadows which seemed to wish to take him somewhere different. This lion was seen by the client as a figure which pointed to an unexplored (yet frightening) realm of possibilities.

1 T: Could I understand where you are then - you felt you were being led away back to - a life-style you didn't want?

2 M: No I saw that as being – this lion that was saying 'look you don't want that' and I knew I didn't but y'know I'm - hm and for a while perhaps I really felt strong that I was doing that but now I feel that I can't do what the lion wants me to do

3 T: What if the lion could talk what would it say to you about that?

4 M: I dunno - perhaps 'Have some courage?' 'Believe in yourself?'

5 T: What has the lion got that you don't have?

6 M: Strength

7 T: Strength - well - if we were to stay with this idea we could say maybe that you're on that roller coaster you can't get off the rails and you're compelled to go where - where wherever the train wants to go because the strength isn't there to get off

8 M: I get confused now - over what's important - is it important to start raking over my past experience or is it more important to express more healing and growth - in other ways I sometimes wonder whether its - whether going over the past is the - the answer - or is it a different experience - I don't know

(T. = Therapist. M. = Mike).

Throughout, the passage is marked by an attempt on the part of the therapist to introduce an irrealistic question in which dream content is used to prompt the client into uncovering hidden resources. Irrealism is a frequently used device in psychotherapy for drawing clients' attention to 'possible worlds' in which new behaviours and new thoughts might become available (Gaik, 1992). The therapist's statement at lines 3 and 5 is both a question and an invitation to follow the lion should it lead somewhere the client might wish to go. This dream figure is next treated by the therapist as literal ('you were being led away'). This implication (i.e. to explore what the lion would suggest) is taken up by the client and expanded upon as having issued a command ('you don't want that'). But nevertheless this imaginary invitation is rejected for reasons of incapacity. The lion-figure is then turned into a metaphorical rather than a dream figure ('what if the lion could talk'). The therapist continues with this trope in an attempt to identify a resource which might be re-accrued to the client ('What has the lion got that you don't have?'). Again, there is a co-operative response which is echoed back by the therapist ('Strength?'). So far the conversational moves appear successful since the client appears to have appropriated the metaphor as a prompt to examine his personal resources. It is only at that point (line 8) that the therapist realises that the client's response refers to the lion in the dream rather than to the client himself and that the metaphor has failed.

In line 7 the therapist re-formulates the dream narrative so that the 'idea' of strength can be trans- ferred from the lion to Mike thus lifting it out from the dream context into the therapeutic one. The shift itself ('well - if we were to stay with this idea') marks a change in talk about the dream to talk about Mike. But the move breaks down immedi- ately after this as the client expresses confusion and changes the subject again, this time with a new question about what it means to do therapy. Interestingly, the force of the question (for the client) is that it is heard as posing a dilemma: should he explore the past in time-honoured therapeutic fashion or should he seek a new kind of 'growth' experience altogether? Thus he introduces a different strand of therapeutic discourse and redirects the conversation in just that way.

Material of this kind, common enough in many therapeutic interviews, draws a line under the explanations of therapeutic discourse we have been examining here. The notion that therapy is a matter of translation from one code into another, or a covert offering of disguised similes, cannot be substantiated unless it is shown that clients are always treating the proffered metaphor in the intended way. But tropes, like jargon, are always liable to be misunderstood, distorted, resisted, reformulated or (as does happen) accepted and absorbed into the therapeutic context. The foregoing analysis is offered as a small example of the vagaries which are mundane features of therapeutic talk.

PSYCHOTHERAPY AS RHETORIC

RHETORIC AND THERAPY - CARL ROGERS - ALBERT ELLIS -
CLOSED CONVERSATIONS IN THERAPY - FORMULATIONS IN
THERAPY - FRITZ PERLS

Cecily: That certainly seems a satisfactory explanation, does it not?

Gwendolen: Yes, dear, if you can believe him.

Cecily: I don't. But that does not affect the wonderful beauty of his answer.

Wilde, 1954. The Importance of Being Earnest.

Rhetoric and therapy

Much of the continuing argument in this chapter is built on the premise that something goes awry when therapists move from text to action, from talk *about* therapy to talk *in* therapy. In the academic environment in which descriptions of psychotherapy are produced and analysed persuasive strategies are employed in order to define what psychotherapy is or what it should be. But the instant practitioners seek to implement these discourses they will have to do a lot of work in order to make them stick. Often, as I seek to show, therapists, particularly those credited with high institutional status, will use rhetoric in order to bring to bear their versions of reality on the client. Such moves, which may entail an intricate management of conversational rules in order to smooth away inconsistencies and disagreement, may come close to erasing the voice of the client.

Earlier, in discussing texts about therapy the opportunity to examine their rhetoric was foregone in order to leave such matters to their proper place. To remind the reader: Lazarus sought to reconcile clinical procedures which were 'scientifically-tested' with those that actually stood a better chance of working; Reich worked to reconcile 'unsystematic' analysis with the 'necessary' one; while Wolpe argued that 'lawful' techniques must be better than 'speculative' intuitions. Further on, we saw Gellner contrasting 'mystical' experiences with 'rational' ones, and Szasz's preference for 'concrete' discourse over 'metaphorical' discourse. Finally, Labov & Fanshel based their analysis of a therapeutic inter-

view on a distinction between 'coherent' and 'incoherent' discourse. But all had in common an
attempt to master problems which arose from
explaining or justifying the processes of
psychotherapy.

One way to unravel the rhetoric of texts which seek
to value one position over another is to use the
method of deconstruction. Derrida has shown us
how arguments of this type are inherently unstable,
resting as they do on binary oppositions in which
one polarity is held to be the 'truth' while the other
is the unwanted, excluded, remainder:

....in a classical philosophical opposition
we are not dealing with a peaceful
coexistence of a vis-a-vis, but rather with a
violent hierarchy. One of the two terms
governs the other (axiologically, logically,
etc.), or has the upper hand. To
deconstruct this opposition, first of all, is to
overturn the hierarchy at a given moment.
(Derrida, 1981: 41)

This privileging of one term over another requires
rhetorical work in order to instantiate the hierarchy,
maintain the selected opposition of terms, and

muddy the argument. Examples of binary oppositions are being/nothing; speech/writing; and
appearance/reality. And, in psychotherapy:
conscious/unconscious; authentic self/false self;
progress/resistance; pathology/cure.

Carl Rogers: Ringing bells in your head

Carl Rogers was influential as the founder of
Person-centred therapy, an (allegedly) non-directive
type of psychotherapy which forms much of the
basis for the world-wide counselling movement
which has grown in strength over the past fifty
years. A key feature of this approach is that the
counsellor offers a position of 'unconditional positive regard' (Rogers, 1967: 47) towards the client in
order to facilitate self-understanding, integration
and self-actualisation. According to Rogers, this is
one of the 'necessary and sufficient' conditions for
therapeutic change. The others are that two persons
be in contact; that the psychotherapist be an inte-
grated person, the therapist experiences 'empathetic
understanding' of the client's position and that the
communication of unconditional positive regard is
achieved at least minimally (Rogers, 1990: 221).

For Rogers, the urge to actualise the self is the most
basic human drive (Rogers, 1990: 236ff). All psychological difficulties are the result of blocks to this

instinctual need. The self is defined as an organism which seeks self-actualisation. The self-concept, by contrast, is based on the introjected judgments about what the self should be. Where the self-concept is identical with the organismic self the individual is held to be congruent; where a discrepancy arises the individual is held to be incongruent. As the self-concept emerges in childhood the individual acquires a further need for unconditional regard (love) in order to identify the organic self with the self-concept. This also entails that the person may introject the attitudes of others in order to secure (conditional) regard from them. Harsh judgments lead to a shrinking of the self-concept and to demanding conditions of self-worth which the person is obliged to fulfil. Moreover, lack of a positive self-evaluation will result in a low-functioning self-concept that restricts the possibility of self-actualisation. An inadequate self-concept leads in turn to denial of any experience which does not match the individual's impoverished conception of the self. This, finally, results in blocks to self-actualisation or to fear, anger, anxiety and depression as the fragile self-concept is endangered.

The Person-centred therapist seeks to restore the client's capacity for self-actualisation by increasing their exposure to unconditional positive regard. The emphasis is on the quality of the relationship to be developed between the two not on any procedures or techniques to be followed by the practitioner. As such the approach is a kind of studied do-nothingism in which the therapist works to exhibit concern, genuineness and congruence and waits for the client's instinctive capacity for actualisation to assert itself (Rogers, 1967: 125ff). As the right attitudes continue to be displayed, Rogers tells us:

Both from my clinical experience and from our research investigations we find that if attitudes of the sort that I have described are present then quite a number of things will happen. She'll explore some of her feelings and attitudes more deeply; she's likely to discover some hidden aspects of herself that she wasn't aware of previously. Feeling herself prized by me it's quite possible she'll come to prize herself more. Feeling that some of her meanings are understood by me then she can more readily perhaps listen to herself, listen to what's going on in her own experience, listen to some of the meanings she hasn't been able to catch before. Perhaps if she senses a realness in me she'll be able to be a little more real within herself.... (Rogers: in Shostrom, 1966).

Rogers further defines psychotherapy here as a process through which clients are in contact with their actual experiences, as opposed to their cognitive distortions about those experiences; a process in which individuals become more authentic, a description couched in characteristically vague terms:

> We are talking about something at an experiential level - a phenomenon which is not easily put into words, and which, if apprehended only at the verbal level, is by that very fact, already distorted. Perhaps if we use several sorts of descriptive formulation, it may ring some bell, however faint, in the reader's experience, and cause him to feel "Oh, now I know, from my own experience, some of what you are talking about." (Rogers, 1967: 103)

In the next extract Rogers identifies the target of psychotherapy. This target is the real, self-actualising subject able to access the meaning of experience in an untrammelled and healthy way. The therapist's authenticity and client's health go together: the therapeutic process of fostering congruence forms a tandem with the natural self hungry for expression and actualisation.

Therapy seems to mean a getting back to basic sensory and visceral experience. Prior to therapy the person is prone to ask himself, often unwittingly, 'What do others think I should do in this situation?" 'What would my parents or my culture want me to do?" 'What do I think ought to be done?" He is thus continually acting in terms of the form which should be imposed upon his behaviour. This does not necessarily mean that he always acts in accord with the opinions of others. He may indeed endeavour to act so as to contradict the expectations of others. He is nevertheless acting in terms of the expectations (often introjected expectations) of others. During the process of therapy the individual comes to ask himself, in regard to ever-widening areas of his life-space, 'How do I experience this?" 'What does it mean to me?" 'If I act in a certain way how do I symbolise the meaning which it will have for me?" He comes to act on a basis of

> what may be termed realism. (Rogers,
> 1967: 103)

The opposition here lies between a personal 'experiential' level of awareness couched in 'sensory and visceral' terms and given the preferential term 'realism' and, by contrast, the undesirable alternative - the 'forms' (or norms) and 'expectations' which are 'imposed' on behaviour. We are told that psychotherapy assists people to pass over from an artificial, judgmental, way of life to a natural existence based on authentic feelings and needs.

The passage skilfully ranks personal experience over the norms of others. Through discourse-in-action the potential client is manoeuvred into acting out the suggestions offered by Rogers. The key trope via which Rogers' performance is managed is that of meiosis in which some proposition is deliberately understated as in Rogers' use of phrases like 'perhaps', 'seems to mean' and 'may be'. Meiosis is a useful way of drawing the client's attention to something without committing the psychotherapist to an outright assertion of fact. A particular type of meiosis, namely a litote, in which the speaker appears to state the reverse of what is intended, (e.g. 'I hear you're not doing so well'), has been found by Bergmann (1992) to feature in psychiatric interviews as a way of drawing the client into scrutiny by stating what ails him. Psychiatrists can understate their knowledge of the case in order to cast 'fishing trips' into the patient's mind. In this way they are able to pitch themselves as open-minded outsiders attempting to gather 'the facts'; a diagnosis of the clinical problem. Meiosis, then, is one way in which a psychological investigation can become intrusive without appearing to be so, thereby exposing clients to the therapeutic gaze.

Let us begin by noting that Rogers straight away offers a difficulty: what he has to say about the therapeutic process 'is not easily put into words' and if the phenomenon is apprehended merely at a verbal level then it will be 'distorted'. In this way Rogers both constructs and then answers a problem: how can private, felt, experience be put into words? The answer is a kind of shotgun approach as 'several' formulations are tried in the hope that the reader will be able to arrive at answers which ring a bell in the head. Circumventing this problem Rogers also raises the stakes: if we are to understand him we must check our own 'experience' in an undistorted way. In somewhat circular fashion, understanding therapy requires that one is able to practice therapy oneself - those who have an 'experience' are already on the way to the desired state of affairs while those who do not are 'distorting' in some way. Here, meioses are employed: 'perhaps' if a certain course is followed 'it may ring some bell, however faint' in the reader's experience.

Such experiences, once elicited from a self-examination, may 'cause him to feel' for himself a sought-for answer which Rogers presents in terms of a script-formulation (an example of something which the client may say to herself). This ploy enables Rogers to avoid specifying the answer himself while shoe-horning the reader towards the correct response. We might note that the second repetition of the word 'experience' has elided the sense of the word in such a way as to make it more likely rather than not that the reader will come up with self-talk which matches Rogers' formulas. The similar noun phrase 'experiential' has been defined in terms of a non-verbal, proprioceptive, response; the first use of the word 'experience' has been employed in the sense of recalling or remembering something; while the second carries the sense of introspecting some internal state of affairs. The very vagueness of signification here - something 'not easily put into words' - makes it harder to pin Rogers down and thus refute him. Were the client try and do so this could mean that he is still acting in terms of 'imposed forms of experience'. The direction to examine oneself becomes still more imperative if this pitfall is to be avoided. Even so, there seems to be an oscillation at work here, one that involves a hermeneutic circle as the reader shuffles back and forth between organismic responses and an interpretation of those responses.

Rogers offers various kinds of script formulations to characterise the sort of self-talk which leads clients into error. Here scripts like 'what do others think I should do?', 'what would my culture want me to do?', 'what do I think ought to be done?' are held up as examples of the kind of things undeveloped, or even disturbed, people might tell themselves before entering into Rogerian therapy. That is: normative or other-directed thinking is contrasted with authentic feelings which clients can unravel for themselves. Subtly, Rogers is inviting us to draw away from the influence of others: of parents, peers and culture, in order to follow *his* directions, without ever making it explicit that this is in fact the case. Again, the use of fictional self-talk can disallow accusations of manipulation while increasing the chances that such generalised formulations will 'ring some bell' in readers' heads. The rhetorical encirclement by which alternatives to Rogers' argument are increasingly disallowed is made yet tighter by the proposition that even where individuals are not acting 'in accord' with the opinions of others or are even endeavouring (no doubt vainly) to 'contradict' such opinions they are 'nevertheless acting in terms

of...introjected expectations'. Metaphors for pre-
therapy conditions, we may also note in passing, are
cast in auditory terms: things put on a verbal level;
bells that ring inside heads; internal questions, while
in the process of therapy this auditory mode trans-
fers to 'ever-widening areas of his life-space' - we
move from an enclosed internal monologue to the
widening space of a therapeutic cure.

Rogers' assertions rest, as we have seen, on a
ranking of authentic (organismic) experiences over
inauthentic ones (cultural norms). But, paradoxically, one can only be known in terms of the other.
We require Rogers' texts - and their circulation in a
cultural order - if we are to make these distinctions.
'Basic' experience, then, requires a textual supplement, as well as the attention of a counsellor, if we
are to get to it. But this authentic personal experience is only identifiable by means of the expertise
of others, or the texts in which it is explained.

Switching now to a brief example of Rogers' counselling technique, we can notice the same rhetoric at
work as it switches to the therapeutic interview. In
what follows we can notice Rogers pursuing the real
subject of therapy - the experiential self - and
opposing it to evaluative norms. Although his initial
formulation is rejected by his client (Gloria) he
succeeds in getting it accepted the second time
around by means of an artful reworking of Gloria's

own definition of her predicament. This negotiation allows Rogers to secure Gloria's acceptance of his approach despite her doubts. The transcript which follows is taken from an educational tape in which Rogers, along with representatives from other therapeutic schools (Albert Ellis and Fritz Perls), was called upon to demonstrate, in a half-hour recording, the workings of Person-centred therapy with Gloria, a volunteer. In a preliminary talk in which he briefly sketches the main tenets of the Person-centred approach, Rogers worries whether he will be able to live up to his own standards. Will he, for example, be able to 'be real in the relationship' (Rogers, in: Shostrom, 1966); will he be 'caring' for her? In connection with his therapeutic aims he asks:

Will I be able to understand the inner world of the individual from the inside? Will I be able to see it through her eyes? Will I be sufficiently sensitive to move around inside the world of her feelings so that I know what it feels like to be her? So that I can sense not only the surface meanings but some of the meanings that lie somewhat underneath the surface? (Transcript from: Shostrom, 1966).

This list of questions indicate the quest which follows, as Rogers digs for the meaning beneath the surface of the client's words and pursues the undistorted, organismic, experiential basis for her predicament.

Gloria begins the interview by telling Rogers she is newly divorced and is experiencing a conflict between her need for relationships with men and her further wish not to upset her nine-year old daughter with news of her sexual adventures. She then describes her guilt over the lies with which she hides this part of her life from her daughter. She asks Rogers to help her be rid of the guilt feelings with which she is troubled; a request he refuses. When he is accused of just sitting there and letting her 'stew on it' he characteristically replies:

Extract 1

Rogers: And I guess I'd like to say 'No - I don't want to just let you stew in your feelings' but on the other hand - I also feel that this is the kind of very private thing that I couldn't possibly answer for you but I sure as anything will try to help you work towards your own answer. I don't know if that makes sense to you but I mean it.

(Transcript from: Shostrom, 1966).

This leads to a further self-examination, on

Gloria's part, of her guilt and more confessions concerning her personal life. During the interchanges she receives several prompts which ask her to consider her predicament as resulting partly from thwarted inner needs and desires. For example, Rogers avers that her difficulty is 'in you as well'. Meanwhile there is a need to 'accept' the actions of the self. Later on the point is repeated: 'you do have these desires you do have these feeling but...you don't feel good about them' because there is a 'feeling that only a part of you is acceptable to anybody else'. The discussion leads by turns to an assertion by Gloria that her guilt arises from childhood experiences and then to some speculations concerning the high personal standards she has set herself:

Extract 2

1 G: I want to do this and it feels right but after all I'm not being a good mother and I want to be both - I'm becoming more and more aware of what a perfectionist I am and that's what it seems like – I wanna be so perfect - either I want to be perfect - in my standards - or not have that need any more

2 R: Or I guess I hear it a little differently - that what you want is to seem perfect - that it means it's - of great - a matter of great importance to you to be a good mother and you want to seem to be a good

mother even if some of your actual feelings differ from that - does that catch it or not?

3 G: Gee I don't feel like I'm saying that - you know? that isn't what I feel really - I want to approve of me always but my actions won't let me. I want to approve of me I - I think

4 R: Do you realise that - all right - let me - I'd like to understand that - you sound as though your actions are kind of outside of you - you want to approve of you but what you do somehow won't let you approve of yourself

5 G: Right

(Transcript from: Shostrom, 1966)

Key: R = Rogers; G = Gloria.

Gloria here sets up a choice which may lead to an answer (of sorts) to her predicament: either to ratchet up her personal conduct so that it meets her perfectionistic standards or to dispense with the standards. Rogers tells her that he hears it differently: what she wants is to seem perfect.

There are some hesitations in speech at this point (line 2), possibly indicative that Rogers is wary of the risk he is taking in offering this formulation. The word 'seem' takes the sense of Gloria's phrase 'want to become perfect' to 'want to seem to be perfect', a very different assertion which is rejected outright (at this stage) by her. Note also the distinction between 'want to seem to be a good mother' and 'actual feelings' (line 2) a split which is consistent with Rogers' theoretical claims. Thus Gloria is, at this stage, being given a tutorial in the Rogerian model. The offer for her to disconfirm this description of her experience - 'does that catch it or not' is taken up with some force and Gloria reasserts her claim that she wholeheartedly wants to be able to approve of herself not just to seem worthy to others. The issue here has much to do with rival definitions of Self. For Gloria there is no split between her approving self and the social self, although there is, perhaps, a difference between the narrative 'I' which seeks approval and the 'me' which engages in therapy. Rogers, meanwhile, continues to work towards his definition of the Self as a Rousseauesque self-actualiser beset by artificial social norms. Although he employs his expert status in order to succeed in his argument he meets with some resistance from Gloria. For that reason he can be read as exercising circumspection in his approach. Referring back to our earlier discussion concerning therapeutic discourse it could be argued that Rogers only succeeds in getting some of his claims accepted at all due to Gloria's willingness to engage in therapeutic discourse in the first place while rejecting (some of) Rogers' assertions in particular cases.

The convoluted use of deixis in line 4 in which the pronoun 'you' is used six times, 'your' is used once and 'yourself' once again works to keep the subject of therapy up for grabs. Note that the first 'you' mentioned refers to the Gloria in front of him while the second indexes the alienated self ('outside of you'). The next 'you' refers again to the speaker in front of Rogers while the fourth 'you' is a narrative self ('you want to approve of you'). The fifth once more documents a split-off, alienated self ('what you do') and the sixth, by contrast, a judging, normative self. Thus Rogers reworking of Gloria's narrative distinctions of self extends into another kind of split, one much more handy for the definitions he wants to work in. He starts by appearing to want to tell her something ('Do you realise that....') then stops, possibly because a straight interpretation would be inconsistent with the non-directive approach he is meant to be demonstrating. He changes this to an undertaking to understand what it is she is saying but this is followed up not with a request for more information but another formulation ('you sound as though your actions are kind of outside you'). Meiosis is used again here ('kind of') and works to mitigate the force of Rogers' claim as does the modaliser 'you sound as though'. Both work also to distance Rogers from the argument should he need to beat another conversational retreat. Notice that Rogers still succeeds in creating a split in the description of Gloria's experience in the same way he did before. First there are the actions going on outside the self in the public arena then there is the 'you that wants to approve of you' - a formulation which is finally accepted by Gloria. It is now open to Rogers to build on the split he has created by reversing it once more so that the alienated 'you' becomes the one with irrepressible organismic needs and the normative 'you' becomes a repository of public standards of conduct. This move occurs approximately one minute further on in the interview shortly after Rogers has got Gloria to agree that her guilt is cutting her off from 'a normal sex life':

Extract 3

1 R: But you really feel that at times you're acting in ways that are not in accord with your own inner standards

2 G: Right - right

3 R: But then we were also saying a minute ago that you can't help that feeling

4 G: I wish I could - that's it - and I can't

(Transcript from: Shostrom, 1966).

Compare this version with that given in line 2 of Extract 2 seen earlier and it can be seen that Rogers has now worked much closer around to defining Gloria's position in ways which lend themselves to his approach. While, to be sure, there is no longer any claim that she just wants to seem to be perfect the claim that she is split between a set of 'actual feelings' which, being natural, she can't help having, and a set of bothersome social norms, remains. We may note also the simplifications in deixis: only three 'yous' are left and all three refer now to the alienated, feeling self which is contrasted to 'your own inner standards'.

Albert Ellis's trained ears

In this section we will look at another example of therapeutic rhetoric which, ironically, contradicts Ellis' claim that his type of therapy frees people from indoctrination. Ellis's argumentative style takes its point of departure from Socratic dialogue and the defeat of irrationality. Yet its application results instead in a substitution of rhetoric for reason imposed by non-rational means. This over-valuation of rationality opens Ellis' practice to a decon-struction which parallels the one elicited from Rogers' work.

Albert Ellis is the founder of the approach known

nowadays as Rational-Emotive Behaviour Therapy (REBT). It is grounded on a distinction between rational and irrational thought. Human beings, according to Ellis, are genetically endowed with the capacity for both. Psychological disturbance arises from the exercise of the latter; mental health from the former (Ellis, 1991: 36). The task of the psychotherapist is to dispute the client's irrational ideas and substitute them with rational ones. The effective therapist, writes Ellis, is a 'counter-propagandist who directly contradicts and denies the self-defeating propaganda and superstitions' of the client (op. cit. p95) and 'who believes wholeheartedly in a most rigorous application of the rules of logic, of straight thinking, and of scientific method to everyday life.' (p103). Propaganda (rhetoric) in favour of this view is necessary because the 'suggestible' individual is often introduced to irrational thinking patterns by 'social propaganda' or 'ideology' (p93).

Neurosis, Ellis tells us, originates in 'fundamentally unsound, irrational ideas' (p93). The characteristics of irrational thought are numerous and inclusive. The therapist fights against 'magical ideas' which are self-destructive, which cater to short-term hedonism, procrastination, are repetitive or resistant to re-learning, superstitious, intolerant, perfectionistic, grandiose, avoidant, or which just haven't been

thought through sufficiently well (Ellis, 1989: 197).
Such ideas are essentially 'insane' as Ellis asserts in
the preliminary to his interview with Gloria:

> ....the individual usually tells himself when
> he's upset - first a sane sentence and then
> an insane sentence - the sane sentence is
> something along the order of 'I don't like
> the thing that I've done' - 'I dislike my own
> behaviour' - and that would be fine but
> unfortunately he follows it with an insane
> sentence which says to himself 'and
> because I don't like my behaviour I am a
> louse I am worthless I am a no-goodnik'
> and this thoroughly insane sentence -
> which is a sentence of faith unfounded on
> fact - which has no empirical reference
> which is a kind of superstitious or
> dogmatically religious system creates what
> we call his anxiety and through his anxiety
> his depression, his guilt, his other forms of
> self-defeatism. (Transcript from: Shostrom,
> 1966)

In the excerpt that follows, Ellis, like Rogers, uses
script formulations to a much greater extent than
Rogers. Here they are offered as examples of the

insane things individuals tell themselves. These depictions of irrational self-talk feature crucially in Ellisian rhetoric as a way of pointing up the contrast between cognitive folly and the sane path that Ellis wants his clients to go along.

The formal basis for REBT is to distinguish between Activating events, Beliefs and (emotional & behavioural) Consequences. In this 'ABC' model the client is taught to distinguish between factual events, the beliefs formed about those events, and the consequences of having those beliefs. They are prevailed upon to actively identify the insane thoughts which give rise to undesired states such as guilt, anxiety and depression. Particular targets are ideas which magnify problems, impose unqualified demands on self or others, presuppose absolute standards of conduct, indulge in wish-fulfilment, or rigidly (and negatively) evaluate events in calamitous ways (Dryden & Gordon, 1990).

The REBT practitioner adopts a particular kind of role in therapeutic interviews: that of the scientifically minded, rational debater who reasons clients out of their illogical or empirically invalid ideas thus convincing them of the paramount need to adopt a rational life-style. In REBT the persuasive task of the therapist is overt rather than disguised. The therapist is a rhetorician and Ellis himself is not slow to own this persuasive role. In a curious turn of logic he claims that by seducing the client he is thereby making them less susceptible to unwanted influences elsewhere:

> This is what the RET therapist 'seduces, cajoles and teaches' most clients to do - to think for themselves, to learn the scientific method and to actively use it for the rest of their lives, and thereby to make themselves less suggestible. (Quoted in Yankura & Dryden, 1994: 105).

In the extract below Gloria's presenting problem is similar to that she provides to Rogers: low self-esteem in relation to male partners and guilt concerning her casual affairs. Ellis then explains that his methods of therapy rest on uncovering the 'simple exclamatory sentences' with which people create their negative emotions. Gloria describes these as having to do with a failure to match up to (male) expectations about her. Ellis tells us that such a sentence on its own would not be enough to cause her shyness and that she must be adding on a further script formulation such as: 'If this is so that would be awful'. Gloria refuses this description and offers an alternative: that in not satisfying potential suitors she has in some way 'missed my chance again'. This move is refused by Ellis who repeats his claim that a sentence of this nature could not be enough to cause her distress and that she must be 'catastrophising' her situation in some other way. It is at this point that we pick up the interview:

1 E: And that's what I call catastrophising - taking a true statement - and there is a good deal of truth in what you're saying - if you didn't get the kind of a man you wanted then it would be inconvenient annoying frustrating - which it really would be and then saying 'I'd never possibly get what I want' and even beyond that you're saying 'and then I couldn't be a happy human being' now aren't you really saying that on some level?

2 G: Yes -

3 E: Well let's just look at that let's just assume the worst as Bertrand Russell once said years ago - assume the worst - that you never got at all for whatever the reasons may be the kind of a man you want - look at all the other things you could do in life to be happy

4 G: Well I - don't like the whole process I don't even like it as I'm going through it I don't - ah all right - even if it wasn't a catastrophe even if I didn't look at it as a catastrophe I don't like the way I'm living right now - for example when I meet somebody I'm interested in that could have some poten-

tial - I find I'm not nearly as relaxed with him - I worry more - 'should I be friendly?' 'should I kiss him goodnight?' 'should I do this?' if it's just a Joe Doe and I don't give a darn I can be anything I wanna be I turn out to be more of a person - when I'm not as concerned - I don't like the way I'm uh - uh well - I seem I'm -

5 E: Uh yeah but you're not really concerned you're over-concerned - you're anxious because if you were just concerned you'd do your best and you could say to yourself 'if I succeed – great - if I don't succeed - tough - right now I won't get what I want' but you're over-concerned or anxious you're really saying again just uh what we said a moment ago 'if I don't get what I want right now I'll never get it and that would be so awful that I've got to get it right now' - that causes the anxiety doesn't it?

6 G: Yeah - or else work toward it

7 E: Yeah but if my -

8 G: If I don't get it right now that's all right but I wanna feel like I'm - working toward it

9 E: Yeah but you wanna guarantee I hear - my trained ears hear you say 'I would like a guarantee of working towards it' and there are no certainties and guarantees

10 G: Well no Doctor Ellis I don't know why I'm

coming out that way what I really mean is I wanna step towards working towards it

11 E: Well - what's stopping you

12 G: I don't know I thought - well what I was hoping is - whatever this is in me - why I don't seem to be attracting these kind of men why I seem more on the defensive why I seem more afraid - you could help me with what it is I'm afraid of so I won't do it so much

12 E: Well my hypothesis is so far that what you're afraid of is - not just failing with this individual man - which is really the the only thing at issue when you go out with a new - man - and we're talking about eligible males now - we'll rule out - the ineligible ones - you're not just afraid that you'll miss this one - you're afraid you'll miss this one and therefore you'll miss every other and therefore you'll prove that you are really not up to getting what you want and - wouldn't − that - be - awful? You're bringing in these catastrophes

(Transcript from: Shostrom, 1966)

Key: E = Ellis; G = Gloria.

Ellis assumes that Gloria is creating catastrophes in her head. Gloria resists this explanation of her problem and offers a counter-proposal of her own, namely that there is something fundamentally inauthentic about the way she is in these encounters. In short, she feels there is something wrong with her, not her thought patterns, and would like to work towards making herself into a different kind of person who might be attractive to the 'right' kind of partner. Ellis' argument is different: her discomfort with men is caused by her false reasoning which gives rise to a worry that she might never find the right man and that if she wants to overcome her fear then it is necessary for her to think in a different way.

Herein lies the difference between them. In Gloria's view her self-doubt is at the core of her problem; for Ellis it is the absence of reason. On these contrary interpretations their conversation founders without ever reconciling their differences.

In this extract, which lasts approximately six minutes in playing time, there are no less than five script formulations: in lines 1 (twice), 5 (twice) and again on line 9. Tag questions are added on twice: 'now aren't you really saying that on some level'? and 'that causes the anxiety doesn't it?'). Tag questions have been identified (Holmes, 1983) as providing opportunities for the listener to confirm or disconfirm the therapist's assertions and so could be understood as offering Gloria the chance to qualify Ellis's claims although, given the frequency with which he uses them, they could be heard as

Ellis insisting on his expert status. On line 4 she claims that catastrophes are not really the issue and on lines 8 and 10 she disqualifies what Ellis says ('or else work toward it') and claims instead that what she really wants is a good relationship and that her fear of not getting one is a side-issue. This in turn leads to Ellis's most forceful attempt to reinstate his claim ('...but you wanna guarantee I hear - my trained ears hear you say 'I would like a guarantee of working towards it') but this only elicits a yet more explicit denial from Gloria ('Well no Doctor Ellis - I don't know why I'm coming out that way....'). He can then be heard as stepping down and taking a back seat on line 11 ('Well - what's stopping you?') whereupon Gloria asks for help with her awkwardness around men ('whatever this is in me'). At once Ellis reinstates his claims to expert knowledge and offers some more examples of insane self-talk for her to consider. The piece starts as it ends, with Ellis insisting that Gloria is cata-strophising her predicament and thereby creating her therapeutic problem that way.

To have a conversation rather than an exchange of monologues it is required that both parties allow themselves to go with the conversation wherever it does, attending mutually to the reflexive force of the other's contributions. It requires, too (Gadamer, 1989) that both parties seek to comprehend the position of the other. But little attendance to these considerations is seen from Ellis' contributions for all his conclusions are quickly settled without much reference to anything Gloria might have to say. Surmises are turned into established facts rapidly and easily by means of rhetoric. In this connection the issue of reality looms large in the excerpt, possibly because the exact status of Ellis' assertions are highly debatable and therefore subject to negotiation and confirmation by Gloria. Thus on line 2 she is told that what she is saying has 'a good deal of truth' in it and that she 'really would be' frustrated by her problem (lines 6-7) before she is asked to agree that there must be something else she is 'really saying' on some other level. Again on lines 5 there is something else she is 'really saying' which causes her anxiety but by line 12 these assertions have been downgraded to a 'hypothesis' possibly due to the impact of Gloria's repeated denials. In this way we note how the downward modalization from what was 'really' said to an educated guess is forced on Ellis by conversational rules of confirmation: each turn in the dialogue offers fresh opportunities for alignment or non-alignment of either party's projects within that same talk and Gloria utilises this feature to vigorously assert her own ideas. Thus Ellisian rhetoric, powerful as it is, is held constantly in check by the rules of conversation.

This is nowhere more so than on lines 9-10:

9 E: Yeah but you wanna guarantee I hear - my trained ears hear you say 'I would like a guarantee of working towards it' and there are no certainties and guarantees

10 G: Well no Doctor Ellis I don't know why I'm coming out that way what I really mean is I wanna step towards working towards it -

Having failed to convince Gloria of the truth of his claims: that she must be creating irrational ideas in her head, Ellis falls back on an indirect assertion of expertise. His expression 'my trained ears' is a synecdoche which means something like 'experienced and knowledgeable clinician whose surmises can be relied on'. The metaphor acts a category entitlement (Potter, 1996b: 132ff) by which Ellis buttresses his argument by virtue of his position as a clinical authority. But there is a paradox here. If the goal of therapy, for Ellis, is to teach individuals 'how to dispute irrational ideas....and to internalize rules of logic and scientific method' (Ellis, 1989: 199) what is the status of Ellis' own ideas? If, in practice his disputational methods rely on poetic fictions and repeated dogmas is there not a curious reversal by which the rational is imposed by means of the non-rational? But there is more:

> The basic tenet of RET is that emotional upsets, as distinguished from feelings of sorrow, regret, annoyance and frustrations, are caused by irrational beliefs. These beliefs are irrational because they magically insist that something in the universe should, ought, or must be different from the way it indubitably is. (Ellis, 1991: 206 - emphasis in original).

But the practice of REBT (like that of all other therapies) could not exist at all unless there were a supply of clients all demanding that they, as individuals, should be different from what they are, or that a portion of the universe should be different from what it actually is. In fact this is precisely Gloria's demand for herself. In offering her some script-formulations to try on for size Ellis seeks her participation in therapy but this, in turn, requires that Gloria's demands for self-change are glossed as unrealistic, exaggerated or irrational. But it is precisely this tendency which has brought her in for therapy. The harder Ellisian rhetoric pushes for rational living the more dependent it becomes on 'irrational' demands for psychotherapy.

Closed conversations in therapy

Therapy-in-action is displayed in conversation. We do not learn about therapy just by studying what therapists say they are doing or by reading texts which theorise about it. Since therapists are implicated in the settings they seek to define and change then 'therapy' will result not only from their participant contributions to talk but the way in which those contributions are redefined by clients as the conversation unfolds. The manoeuvres of the therapist are continually being documented, sometimes favourably and sometimes not, by the client. Referring back to Garfinkel's (1967: 33-4) observations concerning the documentary method, the responses obtained (including silence) are an account of, and a running commentary on, the therapeutic interview. This points to the tacit accountability of therapeutic work, however unwelcome this may be. We have seen how Dean, Rhoda and Gloria can be heard documenting for themselves the meaning of therapy in a variety of ways, not all of which received an adequate response from the therapist. Where this mis-recognition is not accounted for by analysts a category mistake arises in which 'resistant', 'incoherent', 'unhelpful', 'inauthentic' or 'irrational' responses by the client are documented as the stuff of therapy - when they are strictly speaking a situated response to the conversational moves made just within that particular interview. Although these moves and counter-moves may have real consequences outside the interview room (some even beneficial) such events can only be known from their inclusion and interpretation in further conversations between clients and therapists.

If therapists are too doctrinaire in their approach they give up the possibility of a genuine dialogue and turn instead to what Bakhtin terms an *authoritative monologue* (Bialostosky, 1995: 89). It is a monologue whose function is primarily to authorise the academic, medical and professional status of its producer (op. cit. p90-1). And the more authoritative it becomes it risks treating the recipient as an object for analysis and reformation rather than as a person (Shotter, 1993: 62).

Psychotherapists operating from a position of mastery can only maintain this position so long as they ignore the reciprocal quality of therapeutic interviews and the contributions clients bring to it. Inattention to the constructive quality of their interpretations and a certain facility in documenting what is heard as an index for something else ensures that their interpretative efforts run seamlessly into a discourse of mastery. Donald Spence has referred to this phenomenon as 'narrative smoothing'. His analyses of Freud's essays and case-histories (Spence, 1982; 1986) interpret Freud's methods as a re-inscription in which the client's original story is enfolded within the larger narrative which is Freudian theory. He claims that this narrative re-telling works on two levels: the first in which therapists and clients retell the client's story in the consulting room and the second in which therapists present another tale in their published case histories. What is of interest in Spence's account is his retelling of the rhetorical process through which this is accomplished. He refers to 'arbitrary inter-pretations', 'selective reporting', 'omissions', 'narra-tive revision', and 'clarifications' (Spence, 1986: passim) as examples of the way in which therapists' versions of events are constructed:

> This kind of narrative smoothing comes about because we fail to realise that the facts are not fixed, that the referents are never unambiguous, and that each reading will depend on the preconceptions and prejudices of the reader. This kind of narrative smoothing results from a failure to take into account the hermeneutic properties of the clinical account... (Spence, 1986: 213).

In the same way psychotherapists are only able to

document the client's talk as an index of pathology, or the unconscious, or dissociated states, cognitive malfunction, etc. so long as they do two simultaneous and inter-related things. Firstly, to treat clients' statements as symptomatic of some other order of things; and secondly to treat the client's contribution to this process as an unacknowledged resource for what they are doing. Rhetorics of mastery, then, can work only so long as therapists ignore the constructive quality of both their own and the client's interpretations. Expert knowledge in therapy, so-defined, is a function of the conversational materials from which it takes its departure and (when re-inscribed into a text) is an abstraction from the same.

Formulations in therapy

I turn now to the issue of interpretation in therapy. Since the time of Janet and Freud interpretations have been held to be central to the work of the therapist. Indeed, some might argue that is all that therapists ever do; that the only difference between one school of thought and another lies in the interpretations which each has to offer.

However that may be, I am not concerned here with the psychological truth of therapeutic interpretations. My interest lies in how they are worked up in therapy through the use of a conversational device called a formulation.

The specific mechanism by which therapists use ordinary conversation to introduce their interpretations was canvassed in an influential paper by Schwartz (1976) which demonstrates how clients' statements are turned into material for therapy. His point of departure was to consider the problem of how therapists challenge versions of events held by clients without jeopardising their sense of self-determination, or disturbing their trust in the therapist, or breaking the rule that the client's version of events is considered primary. Conversely, he also raises the question how clients carry out the work of psychotherapy. What, he asks, are 'the basic ingredients for a rather general method for changing people's minds?' (Schwartz, 1976: 61).

His answer is that therapists accomplish their aims by the use of a formulation. This is a move in which the gist of what is heard is first summarised in such a way that the client's attention is drawn to the deeper meaning of what has just been said (Potter, 1996b: 48-9). Formulations may be preceded by phrases like 'so what you're saying is...' or 'that sounds to me like…'. They offer an opportunity not only to sum up what has just been said by the other party but also to re-describe the matter in a way which leads to a new direction in therapy.

Psychotherapists typically use formulations to turn the client's attention to the sub-conscious intentions, motives and purposes which lie underneath their assertions. If we follow Schwartz (p59-67) the use of formulations in therapy involves four basic steps:

1 Treat utterances as conversational objects

2 Decide what action is performed by the utterance (i.e. what it 'does' rather than what it 'says')

3 Link speech-act to motive or intention allegedly held by the speaker

4 Offer response which draws attention to motives and intentions underlying the client's actions

We may note that steps 2 and 3 are hermeneutic matters in which the surface meaning of clients' statements are set aside as the therapist looks instead for the reasons why clients act the way they do. As Schwartz points out, this way of treating conversation, in which statements are re-described in terms of intentions and purposes forms an induction into psychotherapy for the newcomer. Novices soon learn to treat their own and others' statements in terms of some underlying psychological reality rather than at face value. This reality, so far as the psychotherapist is concerned, is often a mirror of the naming practices which she learned in the training school. The client too, may already be familiar with such terms as are transmitted through television, books and the agony column: 'damaged bits of the self', unconscious desires, faulty cognitions, low self-esteem, etc. Even so, vocabularies of motive are not the only focus for a formulation. They can also be used to characterise the relationship between therapists and clients or to interpret what each wants from the other (e.g. 'I don't know why I'm coming out that way'). Additionally, metaphors are frequently used inside formulations in a way that makes them more seductive (e.g. 'this sounds like the lion talking...'). It is important to realise that formulations are negotiable instruments which, like metaphors, require hearers to carry out interpretive work - an invitation which may easily meet with a refusal.

A formulation, it may be realised, is only a more explicit form of the documentary method. Psychotherapists document the hidden order of motives and intentions behind their client's statements and they, in turn, take up or turn down the formulation in ways which are further documented by the therapist, and thus furnish the materials for psychotherapy. Likewise, clients may rework the formulation in ways which create new conversational themes for mutual exploration. Neither are doing anything essentially different from participants engaged in everyday conversations except for the fact that, in therapy, formulations are used more systematically as tools for investigating the client's psyche and to fulfil the discursive function of psychotherapy. Yet no more is required to explain how therapists work to change minds than a rule which is employed by countless numbers of people in everyday conversations when they wish to draw attention to matters of mutual interest.

Fritz Perls: Getting hold of the obvious

We now turn to an extract from a further interview with Gloria, this time with Fritz Perls, in which the use of formulations in reinterpreting the clients' statements is further shown. What is also of interest in this interview is the reflexive force of Perl's formulations. For example, he not only formulates Gloria's statements and non-verbal behaviour but also claims that her underlying intentions are directed at him. Thus he characterises Gloria's 'dumb and stupid' behaviour as a ploy which forces him to be 'more explicit' while her 'phoniness' is a 'bluff' which disguises her real emotions. However, since it is only Gloria's intentions which are examined while her critique of Perls' intentions are disallowed the resemblance to dialogue is superficial. The denial of reciprocal rights imparts a certain alienating quality to the exchange which is recognised in despairing fashion by Gloria. Perls' position as an expert remains inviolate and so, despite its resemblance to a conversation, his work here demonstrates unreflective mastery in action.

Frederick (Fritz) Perls, like many other therapists of his generation, was originally trained as a psychoanalyst. During the 1940s he began to move away from psychoanalysis for reasons he gives in a book he co-authored in 1951: *Gestalt Therapy*. Perls's rejected the notion of an Unconscious Mind and the corresponding theory of repression and substituted the Unconscious with a field of 'contact boundaries' (Perls, et. al. 1973: 273-282). These boundaries are permeable zones of interaction between the organism and its environment or between one organism and another. In these fields organic needs (e.g. emotions) come to the fore and form a figure (of concern) which is highlighted against a contextual ground (e.g. aggression from another). This figure/ground configuration is what is meant by a gestalt, a term loosely borrowed from gestalt psychologists such as Koffka, Kohler & Wertheimer (Clarkson, 1989: 4). An example of such a gestalt in therapy would be a client uncovering her emotions over a dead parent where before the source of her grief had not been apparent.

Each gestalt requires closure so that the need associated with it can be satisfied and the organism moves on to form new gestalts. It should be added that a gestalt may be instinctive, mental, or emotional and may arise in a social or personal context, or in dreams and fantasy. Blocks to closure arise from a failure to distinguish between what belongs to the organism and what to the environment. For example, the individual may introject ideas or feelings from others as if they belonged to the self; or project a personal need onto someone else and thus disown it. Where this occurs a split arises and unfinished concerns form alienated parts of the self awaiting resolution (Perls, 1969: 10). Following Reich the organism is understood as powered by vital energy which insists on attempting to close out its gestalts in action, in speech, in dreams or - if thwarted - in neurosis. One important reason Gestalt psychotherapy utilises frustration as a tool in therapeutic work is that it seeks to 'mobilise' enough energy (op. cit. p32) to break through the 'unfinished situation' (p42) and close out the gestalt. According to Perls (p25ff) Gestalt therapy encourages a process of 'maturation' in which the unsatisfied needs bound up in estranged parts of the self can be recovered and the individual learns to acknowledge and incorporate them, no matter how socially or morally undesirable they may seem. Parallel with this is a further movement towards becoming less dependent on others to fulfil their organic needs. In this way clients learn authenticity, self-acceptance and self-reliance.

In remarks which form a preface to the interview Perls refers to the situated style of the Gestalt therapist's approach:

> In contrast to depth psychology we try to get hold of the obvious - of the surface - of the situation in which we find ourselves and to develop the emerging gestalt strictly on the I and Thou here and now basis. (Transcript from: Shostrom, 1966).

Thus Gestalt therapists recognise, crucially, their own contribution to the client's configuration of the session. Perls, like Reich, advocates that therapists should work with the 'obvious' - with each communication, verbal or non-verbal, which the client makes to the therapist. Gestalt work then is ostensibly built on a recognition of the Other - the 'Thou' and ostensibly pays close attention to the way in which the client's concerns emerge on encountering the therapist. It is an approach which (theoretically) avoids imposing interpretations on the client but instead seeks to bring home the client's organic needs in awareness:

> The basic technique is this: not to explain

things to the client but to provide opportunities to understand and discover himself. For this purpose I manipulate and frustrate the client in such a way that he is confronting himself. In this process he identifies with his worst potential - for instance through assimilating his projections by acting out - by acting out the alien parts of himself. Principally I consider any interpretation to be a therapeutic mistake as this would imply that the therapist understands the client better than the client himself. (Transcript from: Shostrom, 1966).

In the excerpt which follows it is certainly possible to see Perls carrying out the aim of frustrating Gloria. Throughout we notice Perls getting hold of the obvious: Gloria's grimaces, foot movements, smiles and conversational asides, although he is by no means averse to interpretations – using formulations at every turn.

The first excerpt occurs approximately three minutes into the interview. At the commencement of their talk Gloria complains of feeling 'scared' to which Perls responds by drawing attention to her expression and querying how it is possible for her to be afraid while smiling. She explains the laugh, plausibly enough, as a 'cover' for her fear. Her fears are thereupon explored and Gloria relates them to Perls himself. The excerpt takes up the conversation at this point.

Extract 1

1 Perls: Now what can I do to you?

2 Gloria: You can't do anything but I can sure feel dumb and I can feel stupid for not having the right answers! -

3 Perls: Now what would it do to you to feel dumb and stupid? -

4 Gloria: I hate it when I'm stupid -

5 Perls: What would it do for you to feel dumb and stupid? I'll put it so - like this - what would it do to - me - if you were to play dumb and stupid?

6 Gloria: That makes you all the smarter and all the higher above me then I really would have to look up to you cos you're so smart you know?

7 Perls: Oh Ja and butter me up right and left right and left - mm-hm -

8 Gloria: No I think you can do that all by yourself!

9 Perls: Uh – I think the other way around - if you

play dumb and stupid you force me to be more
explicit

10 Gloria: That's been said to me before but I don't
buy it - I don't -

11 Perls: Now what are you doing with your with
your feet now?

12 Gloria: Wiggling [laughs]

13 Perls: [laughs] What's the joke now?

14 Gloria: [laughs] Oh I'm afraid you're going to
notice everything I do - gee -

15 Perls: You don't want me to?

16 Gloria: Ah I want you to help me become more
relaxed - yes - I don't want to be so defensive with
you I don't like to feel so defensive - um - you're
acting like - you're treating me as if I'm stronger
than I am and I want you to - protect me more and
be nicer to me -

17 Perls: Are you aware of your smile? You don't
believe a word of it

18 Gloria: [laughs] it's true! But I know you're going
to pick on me for it -

19 Perls: Sure - you're a bluff - you're a
phoney

20 Gloria: Do you believe - you're meaning that seriously?

21 Perls: Yeah - if you say you're afraid and you laugh and you giggle and you squirm - it's it's phoney - you put on a performance for me

22 Gloria: Oh I – resent that – very much!

23 Perls: Can you express it?

24 Gloria: Yes sir! I am most certainly not – being - being phoney! I - I will admit this - it's hard for me to show my embarrassment and I hate to be embarrassed - boy I resent you calling me a phoney - just because I smile when I'm embarrassed or I'm put in a corner doesn't mean I'm being a phoney

25 Perls: Wonderful - thank you - you didn't smile for the last minute

(Transcript from: Shostrom, 1966).

On lines 3-5 Perls elides from Gloria's thinking that she might feel dumb in front of him to her 'playing' dumb, and follows up with two questions: what would that do for her? And what would that do to him? Remarkably quickly (less than two minutes from first sitting down with her, Perls has brought Gloria under his gaze and introduced her to the presuppositions of Gestalt therapy, that all feeling states are powering the person up towards an action aimed at the environment, in this case Perls himself. In line with the rules of Gestalt therapy he wants Gloria to 'own' this state and interpret it for herself even though the idea comes from him not from her.

Gloria does not take up the hint and continues to talk about Perls himself rather than about what Perls wants her to talk about. This is clearly unsatisfactory and Perls then breaks his own rule and 'interprets' for her on line 9 where he formulates her behaviour as forcing him to be more explicit, making therapy a much less confessional venture than he would like. But his formulation is disconfirmed by Gloria on line 10 ('I don't buy it'), a reply cut off in mid-sentence as Perls draws attention to another to-be-documented social action, namely, what she is 'doing' with her feet. No sooner has she answered that question (ironically?) then Perls switches attention to another piece of her behaviour, this time her smile. His insistence on singling out her speech and behaviour as actions to be uncovered for hidden motives has so far been remorseless but it never at any point in the interview secures Gloria's acceptance.

Throughout Perls follows Schwartz's formula in step-by-step order. First he treats Gloria's words or her behaviour as an object for discussion; then he asks her to describe the action performed by those statements (or does it himself); next he provides her with a motive for the action, which thereupon becomes the material for therapy. But these moves are heard as aggressive, one reason for the acrimonious dispute which occupies most of the interview.

On line 14 Gloria complains that he is commenting on everything she does and thus forcing her on the defensive. This is followed by a request that he be 'nice' to her, a request ignored by Perls, who now draws attention to her smile and tells her (line 17) that she doesn't 'believe a word of it'. He then formulates her actions as 'phoney' (line 19) a move she meets with initial disbelief before losing her temper. By this point Perls has broken one of the unspoken rules of ordinary conversation (at least in the USA) in which repeated questions about what people 'really' mean can cause offence. As Garfinkel observes (1967: 38ff) doing so can be heard as either humorous or as aggressive. In this case Gloria takes Perls' comments on her mannerisms in the ordinary way as a personal attack.

Not all Perls' interventions are strictly formulations, however and it is useful to make some finer distinctions here if we are to distinguish between conversational moves which act in an interpretative sense, and those which act to control the conversation. Hak & de Boer make a valuable distinction in this connection between formulations, interruptions and transformations. An interruption is defined as a move which breaks into the client's sentences in order to change the subject to something else the consultant wants to know about (Hak & de Boer, 1995: 343). We can see Perls doing this on line 11 where he interrupts Gloria's explanation and asks what she is 'doing' with her feet. A transformation is a conversational move which arbitrarily reinterprets something the client has said using what I have called a rhetoric of mastery but which Hak & de Boer term 'another language' (op. cit. p349). An example occurs in line 17 where Perls asserts that her smile denotes insincerity.

Hak and de Boer argue that while formulations are devices associated with psychotherapy the associated forms of interruption and transformation occur more frequently in medical and psychiatric interviews which strip away the life-world context from which the client is speaking in order to quickly move on to diagnosis and evaluation (p342-3). In this connection it is worth recalling that Perls originally trained as a medical doctor and, for a while, practised as a psychiatrist in Frankfurt in the 1920s.

Returning to Hak and De Boer for a moment they comment that in mainstream psychotherapy formulations, when they are attended to by both parties, work to mutually define the 'problem at hand' and the 'shared outcome of the interview' (p353):

...the patient is conceived of as a co-worker, whose consent is necessary for the psychotherapeutic intervention. This implies that the patient must be aware of and needs to have an entrance to the professional voice. By showing how everyday biographical events are translated into professional interpretations, the patient learns what interpretations the professional will make out of his or her talk. (ibid.)

In this extract, therefore, we can see Perls using formulations, interruptions and transformations in ways which exemplify his expert position. This invites strong resistance from Gloria and the result is therapy of a kind which is indistinguishable from a row. She complains that he is acting like he knows 'all the answers' while ignoring her explanations. Perls' formulations challenge the client's social competence, thereby breaking a tacit co-operation principle. When used in this way, it should be realised, they effectively treat the client as an object for analysis rather than as an Other like oneself. To avoid this outcome requires careful contextualisation for each formulation if the client is to document them as prompts for self-examination rather than as arbitrary opinions and requires, also, unremitting attention to the client's orientation to the conversation as 'therapeutic' rather than 'ordinary'.

Gloria's rebuttals are reformulated as types of social action which require further examination by her. Whenever Gloria draws attention to *his* actions and motives Perls formulates her protests as yet more conversational objects to be examined for their underlying motives. That is, he treats her utterances not only as an index for something else but as self-reflexive: the statements are about her, not about him. However, this reflexive quality is denied for his own statements:

Extract 2

1 Gloria: I still think you're judgmental - do you know what? - I have a feeling – you've never felt this way in your life – you feel so secure that you don't have to feel - anybody that does something like this you're going to pass judgement on their being a phoney - well I resent it

2 Perls: Good - now play Fritz passing judgement

3 Gloria: You're on! You're sitting up there in your big old chair

4 Perls: Play it - 'I am Fritz - I pass judgment' - pass judgement on me now

5 Gloria: I don't feel close to you at all Doctor Perls
- I feel that's phoney - I feel like you're playing one
big game -

6 P: Right - sure we're playing games but in spite of
the games I think I've touched you now and then

(Transcript from: Shostrom, 1966).

On line 3 Gloria takes up the (misunderstood) invitation to role-play Perls himself by a vigorous
expression of complaint which is interrupted by
Perls as not conforming with his instructions. She is
to act out the Perls she perceives not the Perls actually in front of her. Perls' contribution to her anger
is denied and her statements about him are treated
as statements about her. This turnaround in the
target of her complaint meets with the new protest
that Perls does not take her seriously. His denial of
her conversational right to formulate his strategy as
judgmental leads her to claim that what they are
having is not a conversation at all but a game. What
is more, she claims, it is now he who is phoney so
long as he refuses to come out and meet her. While
all this may be therapeutic in some way it entails
that Perls himself is missing from the exchange. In
his place is a cipher and Gloria cannot get close to
him at all:

Extract 3

1 Perls: Well I felt you came out quite a bit

2 Gloria: No - I'm mad at ya

3 Perls: Wonderful

4 Gloria: But you seem so detached – you don't even - seem to care that I'm mad at you - it's like you're not recognising me at all Doctor Perls - not a bit!

5 Perls: This is quite true - our contact is much too superficial to be involved in caring - I care for you as far as [indecipherable] you are right now my client - I care for you as I like to - like an artist - to bring something out which is hidden in you – this is as far as I care

6 Gloria: Well I'd like you to - I'd like to feel that there's some - it's frustrating - if I were to leave you right now and not see you again it would frustrate me to feel - like there hadn't been more contact - I feel completely out of contact with you - like I'm talking to the baby that doesn't understand me or something like that - I don't feel we're a bit in contact and it - ooo! that frustrates me

(Transcript from: Shostrom, 1966).

This is the last time we will hear from Gloria in these pages and it seems fitting that we should end with her perceptive commentary on the alienating effect produced by at least one therapeutic exchange. Throughout the interviews she emerges as a witty and perceptive critic of the therapies offered to her. Perhaps her final lesson is that psychotherapists who hide behind their theories while superficially seeking to hold a conversation are too easily picked off by their clients.

5

PSYCHOTHERAPY AS CONVERSATION

THERAPEUTIC CONVERSATIONS - GADAMER AND
HERMENEUTICS - GADAMER AND PSYCHOTHERAPY - OPEN
CONVERSATIONS

---

*Thus a genuine conversation is never the one we
wanted to conduct.* Gadamer, 1989: 383

Therapeutic conversations

In this chapter I argue that not only is therapy a
type of conversation but that it cannot, and ought
not to be, anything else.

What I have sought to show in this book so far is
that psychotherapy must always take place under
conversational rules, which regulate turn-taking, the
length of pauses, expression of emotion, the recep-
tion of interpretations, attention to metaphor and,

above all, the right to ignore, defer, refute or counter-argue the assertions of either party. This last right is particularly relevant to psychotherapy in that it is an unspoken rule that clients should have the final say on versions of events.

Psychotherapy is, however, a conversation of a peculiar type: that is it is both a *hermeneutic* and a *dialectical* exchange.

By *hermeneutic* I mean that therapists use *interpretations* of different kinds which prompt clients to reconsider their positions. Such interpretations may arise from the theoretical model in which the therapist was originally trained and, where this is so, it will reach back to larger discourses of different kinds - medical, scientific, therapeutic, sexual, cultural, social and so forth. The technical device of a *formulation*, is, as I have explained, the device through which interpretations are presented spontaneously in a therapeutic conversation (in 'closed conversations' they may be delivered without preamble using an 'expert voice').

However interpretations can take a looser, everyday form and are contained in anecdotes, analogies, allusions and suggestions, to name just a few. These informal styles have a deeper significance in that they point to the experienced therapist's facility in holding different types of conversation ranging from the theoretical, technical style at one end of the spectrum to the informal, everyday style at the other. At the same time clients will also be using interpretations of their own, both to explain their own predicament and to interpret whatever therapists have to say to them. This to-and-fro of interpretation and re-interpretation leading sometimes to a synthesis of ideas is what is meant by *dialectic* and it is this which is properly speaking, the material of psychotherapy.

However, the dialectic we find in therapy is of a peculiar kind: namely, that it is attended to subjectively by clients. Assuming that the therapist is heard to be offering them interpretations which are sincere, relevant, intelligible and insightful (Grice, 1989: 22-40) the client will seek to apply the offering to her own life. That is to say, she will not be concerned with its objective truth so much as whether it helps her to go on in a different way (Wittgenstein, 1966: 44-45).

Near the start of this book I cited texts by Wilhelm Reich and Arnold Lazarus which pointed to the 'anything-goes' quality of therapeutic interpretations and treatment choices in which those same interpretations and choices were prompted by the client sitting before them. I argued then and elsewhere in this book that many experienced therapists, in practice, do not employ textbook methods in therapy but instead act as 'authentic chameleons', using all their arts of persuasion in order to bring clients round to a particular point of view, or to secure their agreement to trying out a procedure on a trial-and-error basis. In my analysis of a variety of therapeutic interviews, particularly those with Gloria, I demonstrated that therapists who try too hard to impose a method on clients frequently come undone because the conversational rules of therapeutic conversations will always leave the client as the final arbiter on whether they can proceed or not. Although a minority of clients may blindly submit to indoctrination the majority (assuming they do not misunderstand what the therapist is trying to say) will respond on a spectrum ranging from enthusiastic acceptance to outright rejection.

In the examples of therapeutic conversations analysed so far the formulations (interpretations) employed have sometimes been pragmatic (drawing attention to intentions and motives), sometimes theoretical (referring back to psychological theories), sometimes speculative; sometimes as an exercise of authority and occasionally as all four. Other devices have also been used in pursuit of therapeutic ends: metaphors, stories, explanations, script-formulations, tag questions and so forth. In return a variety of responses were elicited: angry, humorous, ironic, resistant, helpful, uninterested, perplexed, etc. Occasionally these have led to new directions in talk but just as often they have come to a conversational dead-end. But, inescapably, the cycle of interpretation-response-reinterpretation has involved active voices constantly seeking to formulate the position from which the other is speaking. It is these continual uncertainties in interpretation which make it so difficult to analyse psychotherapy as process and outcome, or as a formal method.

Using Gadamer's work on hermeneutics I offer a model of psychotherapy which accepts these conversational uncertainties as a given. In so doing I seek to resolve the questions raised from the beginning of this work concerning the relationship between theory and practice and the uncertainties generated by a comparison between talk *about* therapy to talk *in* therapy. Fundamentally Gadamer helps to understand why psychotherapy cannot ever be a formal method (i.e. a science) and why, also, accepting and understanding why this is the case shows us how a non-methodical (or semi-methodical) approach could work.

Gadamer and hermeneutics

Most dictionary definitions define hermeneutics as the study of texts and their interpretations and, by extension, the art of interpretation. However, in modern philosophy, hermeneutics is the investigation of what makes understanding possible. In doing so it raises a reflexive question: what legitimates *my* understanding over other potential interpretations of the same thing? This question is important because in hermeneutics it is a given that no interpretation can ever be final: our enquiries take the form of a conversation which is always *on the way* to truth. One such contribution, which is widely regarded as the most important work on hermeneutics in the 20th Century, is *Truth and Method* by Hans-Georg Gadamer (1960).

Gadamer (1900-2002) was a pupil of Heidegger who, before he wrote *Being and Time*, was a specialist in hermeneutics. However, in Heidegger's lectures on the subject in the 1920s (Heidegger, 1988) hermeneutics is a process through which we examine the pre-conditions required for us to understand and engage in anything at all. Heidegger locates this in *Dasein* - the being we become in any given situation. For example, in writing this book I become an author and call upon the instruments of authorship: laptops, writing programs, books and papers, notes and so forth. Further back, I participate in an art-form which stretches back 2,800 years or so. Going forward, I anticipate the readers who may want to read this work. At my desk I am absorbed in this temporary way of being. Shortly, this *Dasein* will be superseded by another way of being when I go out to dinner with my wife and a few friends. And that activity, too, will have historical precedents, current practices and objectives which go to make it what it is. Our examination of *Dasein's* facticity - of all these prior conditions which make each *Dasein* possible - is, for Heidegger, what is meant by hermeneutics.

In his own philosophy Gadamer retains this onto-logical emphasis on the *Dasein* (what he calls 'the horizon') of the interpreter and the key idea that this way of being is shaped by the practices (including discourses) in which it is engaged. Inter-pretations, therefore, are not personal: they emerge from Dasein's interaction with its subject matter, just as 'therapy' emerges from the interaction of one client with one therapist in a setting with a long history of prior rules of engagement.

In *Truth and Method* Gadamer offers a model of hermeneutics via a wide-ranging survey of art, ethics, jurisprudence, philosophy and the human sciences. In his later years he became interested in psychotherapy and debated whether therapy was a scientific method or a conversational art (Gadamer, 1983). In the brief summary that follows I will discuss those aspects of Gadamer's philosophy which have most relevance to psychotherapy.

The major question that Gadamer seeks to resolve is given in the title of his major work. Can truth in the human sciences be disclosed by following an 'objective' method, such as those employed in historical research, legal investigations, medicine, psychology, psychotherapy and in some types of philosophy? Or, in seeking to understand other human beings and their activities are we always limited by the subjective prejudices we bring to bear on the investigation? For example, a historian investigating a Renaissance dream-book will come across many interpretations of dreams that seem strange to us in the post-Freudian 21st century. How, then, are we to understand a book that tells us that in dreams the soul vacates the body and that dreams are supernatural allegories? A methodical interpretation might explain such theories in terms of their cultural and historical background but in doing so does it really help us to understand the experience of having such a dream in the 16th century? To enter into such an experience would entail our giving up our 21st century perspective, which was the very perspective which launched our enquiry in the first place. In this way one 'horizon', or way of

being in the world, meets another. The understanding that we reach is a result of this dialogue
between two horizons. The result - if the inquiry is
genuinely pursued - will be a partial 'fusion of horizons' which discloses something more about that
which we seek to understand but which is always
limited by the prejudices (pre-judgments) we bring
to the task.

For Gadamer prejudices are not bad or avoidable:
they are a condition of our search for understanding. Without a prejudice in favour of emancipation
from suffering, for example, no one would ever seek
to be a psychotherapist. Prejudices are only problematic when they are forgotten about and become
a cue for mastery and control rather than open-
ended enquiry. We must always bear in mind that
we can never be free of the interpretations that are
embedded in our culture, our society, our personal
history and in the method we select for inquiry. The
best we can hope for is that our horizons will always
go on expanding, that we will become more aware
of our pre-judgments, and that we will achieve a
better understanding of the way in which other
people (in ages past or in the present age) come to
their findings.

The hermeneutic perspective sets limits to the reach
of scientific method both in general and in its application to the study of human beings. Science in

general notices regularities in the observed facts and seeks to explain those regularities by means of theories. History shows that science is always changing both according to new facts that emerge and in terms of the theories which explain them. Physics, for example, has evolved from Newton's mathematical model of planetary motion in the 17th century to current models of quantum mechanics. Interpretations that were considered final three hundred years ago have been found wanting as technology reveals fresh information about the behaviour of sub-atomic particles and new interpretations have emerged which seek to explain those facts. In this way science is always on the way to more and more complete explanations as older interpretations are found wanting.

In the human sciences interpretations are more problematic due to four inter-related factors:

a) the interpersonal, cultural and social rules which form the context of human agency

b) The complex mix of memories, desires, instincts, cognitions, emotions and motives which drive our actions

c) The influence of conscious and unconscious prejudices on our interpretations of the reasons for human activity

d) The limitations of the methods selected for the purpose of study

The interaction of all these factors means that studies of human activities must always be partial, incomplete, time-bound and dependent on the horizon of the observer. Finally, it makes the use of method in the human sciences extremely problematic and a 'science' of psychology impossible.

In Chapter One I briefly discussed the enormous difficulties in carrying out research into psychotherapy and pointed to the paradoxical conclusions reached by quantitative analyses of process and outcome in psychotherapy. I hope I have done enough to show that this type of analysis is entirely unsuited to the investigation of psychotherapy. It is my belief that the only possible method through which psychotherapy could be properly understood is an exhaustive analysis of individual therapeutic interviews aided, whenever feasible, by further interviews with participating therapists and clients invited to discuss the interpretations of the observer. It need hardly be said that this would be enormously expensive as well as ethically impractical.

In my analysis of the Gloria interviews I employed a loose combination of discourse and conversation analysis and this method, too, has obvious limitations. For one thing, I am a psychotherapist myself with my own prejudices about the purpose and conduct of therapy; for another the research was carried out in the aim of formulating an argument for this book. Another, still, belongs to the limitations of those two methods taken together. But the most significant deficit is that I have never met Gloria or her therapists. Had I had the opportunity of meeting her, along with Carl Rogers, Albert Ellis and Fritz Perls, I might have been able to move towards a more complete interpretation of the content and context of their interactions and which, along the way, might also have negated some of my original surmises. But even if I had developed a more complete set of interpretations based on these 'fusions of horizons' I would still have to submit those same interpretations in this book, which would require appropriation and dissent from the horizon of, you, the reader. Which would take us forward to the next stage in this dialectic - a dialectic which began in a conversation between a client and a therapist and which continues in our debate about what exactly happened during that conversation.

Related to these difficulties are the problems I have raised in earlier chapters concerning the 'science' of psychotherapy. If there cannot be a transcendental, objective, standpoint from which therapists explain the actions of their clients then, neither, can there ever be a scientific theory based on those explanations - based, as they are, on intersubjective transactions between therapists and clients.

Freud's call for therapists to undergo psychotherapy before they are qualified for practice (Freud, 1912) in order to purge themselves from from distortions of judgment in their professional interpretations, is merely a repetition of this illusion of a complete theory in which the observer attains complete objectivity concerning another. An illusion, moreover, that invites the counter-argument that therapy and training in psychotherapy are equivalent to an indoctrination in the method (see page 72 earlier in this book).

Gadamer and psychotherapy

Suppose we consider psychotherapy as a hermeneutic art which becomes relevant for those whose life projects have broken down and whose current project is to find their way back to health. If we follow Heidegger and Gadamer we can understand their predicament as one in which their existence has become in some degree strange to them and the self a source of puzzlement. In this alienation from the everyday their actions seem unaccountable precisely because things do not work as they should: they are 'lost'. Conventionally, the client may be anxious, depressed, addicted, stressed, etc. But the source of his distress does not lie in his diagnosis, which is merely the effect, not the cause. His distress lies deeper: in his memories, his unsatisfactory experiences, his confusion and despair, and in his relationship to himself and his relationships with others. He can longer find his way about and so he re-commences his search for a better life.

> Psychotherapy is a form of practical philosophy. It does not draw upon ontology or metaphysics but concerns itself with what is good – or right – in human affairs. (Gadamer, 1983: 119)

The ethical point is directly related to what follows in this paragraph. If psychotherapy aims at disengagement, re-assessment and renewal, then, perforce, it seeks to change the horizon of the client to a more inclusive view. However, if we accept what Gadamer has to say on changing horizons then we come up against the problem of how therapists are to accomplish this given that they are in the same predicament as the client. That is to say that they, too, are bounded by their own horizons, by *Dasein*, by language, by discourse. And their interpretations will share in the incomplete, partial, fallible, finite quality of their clients' interpretations. How, then, is the therapist's view better than the client's?

There are three answers one can give to this question; one strictly professional and two less so. The first is that psychotherapists' rely on their professional training in order to understand their clients' predicaments and give advice. Such advice and help can be salutary. However, for reasons I discussed in Chapter 1 the method in which a psychotherapist has been trained cannot be the sole source of success.

The second answer is that therapists, if they persevere for long enough, will garner a wealth of experience in different therapeutic approaches, mental health problems, and in managing clients from all walks of life (even more so if they had a lot of life experience before training as therapists). It is this deep repertoire of experiences, both in and outside therapy, which give weight to their insights, interpretations and advice.

The wisdom therapists have to offer may not differ very much from that of a wise and trusted friend, particularly if that friend has known us a long time - which gives weight to the argument that therapists are "professional friends" whose successes rely on non-specific factors such as trust, warmth, empathy and social support (see Chapter 1). However, if gifted friends are in short supply an experienced therapist may be your best alternative.

However, there is a third way in which experienced psychotherapists may be more skilled than their non-professional counterparts. And that lies in the art of conversation. It could hardly be otherwise if one has conducted many thousands of hours in therapeutic interviews with people from many different backgrounds expressing the many different problems life has to offer.

This art of conversation has two dimensions. The first belongs to ordinary conversation: skill in the use of stories, metaphors, jokes, allusions and arguments and the like. Along with technical proficiency in the use of formulations, scripts, footings, tag-questions and interactional controls within the therapeutic interview. So much forms the rhetoric of therapy and its persuasive force.

However this art of persuasion relies implicitly on the basic rule of conversation, which is that it is a reciprocal exchange. Which brings us back to what Gadamer has to say about therapeutic conversations.

One useful distinction made by Gadamer is that between a conversation and an examination. In an examination it is taken for granted that the practitioner's view is more authoritative than the receiver's. Such is the case in many types of judicial, medical and psychiatric interviews. These lead to 'closed conversations' in which the voice of the practitioner is dominant. The tell-tale sign, for Gadamer, that we are pursuing an examination rather than a conversation is that our questions are concerned only with right or wrong answers rather than a reciprocal exchange of views. A good example of a closed conversation was given on page 61 in the exchange between Dean and his psychiatrist.

In a true conversation the answers are uncovered by the mutual work of participants. The search for enlightenment is always marked by partiality and from time to time requires that either or both parties make explicit the basis for their interpretations (Gadamer, 1989: 363-4). More profoundly, an inquiry into the real meaning of what clients say entails that therapists seek to position themselves in the horizon from which the client is speaking. But this move towards the other is bound to result in further uncertainty since this fusion of horizons means that one 'falls into' conversation rather than directing it: both parties are led by the talk as mutually created. It is for that reason that all true conversations, for Gadamer, are unpredictable and, during their course, must deviate from the one that either party had planned at the start.

A second pitfall is directly related to the over-use of method in therapy: 'examinations' by 'experts' lead by subtle steps to therapy as indoctrination. I have previously discussed this pitfall in detail both in the prior section on therapeutic discourse and in this section and I refer the reader to those discussions. However, there are some additional remarks I would like to add here which derive from Gadamer's views on the pitfalls in applying methods to human affairs.

The danger of method in psychotherapy is that a course of therapy may not result in health but in agreement with the method. The danger can only be avoided by reversing this procedure and, instead of applying methods to the individual case, we should apply the individual case to the method (Caputo, 2018: 227). In that way each case asks a question of the method rather than taking final answers from it and each case offers an opportunity to enlarge the scope of the method. Paradoxically, it is our 'resistant' clients who show us the pitfalls in our methods and assumptions and offer us an opportunity to broaden our horizons. At bottom, therapy must always keep in view the individual case rather than generalisations about pathology:

> Depression' is not one thing but a
> shorthand for a number of related
> pathologies; even when a particular form
> of depression is diagnosed, the focus of the
> treatment is the individual not just the
> disease (Caputo, 2018: 228)

Another way of putting this same point is that the danger lies in looking *at* the client when we should be looking *with* the client at his predicament.

The third pitfall is that in treating the client's statements as misguided or incomplete therapists (as well as analysts) lose sight of the client's 'otherness' - or the *Dasein* - in which he operates. In such cases there is no true merger of horizons for the simple reason that the therapist never allows herself to be challenged by anything the client has to say. The loss of this recognition leads straight to an examination in which the client's utterances are treated as indices for the presence/absence of some theoretical order of things: organic selves, rationality, gestalts, the missing object, etc. This failure of interchange leads also to the 'narrative smoothing' of accounts mentioned earlier.

This loss of subjectivity can only be restored, if we follow Gadamer, by treating therapeutic conversations as a dialogue in which the 'I' of the therapist seeks to place itself in the 'Thou' of the client. This course seeks to discover the horizon of the client at the cost of setting aside the exclusive horizon of the therapist. But to carry through this 'fusion of horizons' (a metaphor which, for Gadamer, is synonymous with the act of understanding itself) requires that the therapist is able to position herself as working from a limited, finite and fallible perspective. She acknowledges the historically-conditioned and discursive origin of her interpretations and adopts an ironical attitude towards them rather than allowing herself or the client to be bound by them. Note that this strategy carries the implication that from time to time the therapist must step down from her expert position and allow the client to assume the direction of the conversation once it has been noticed that the flow of dialectic has broken down.

Open conversations in psychotherapy

The course of a conversation may be straight and smooth and almost formulaic, as in some call exchanges and medical interviews. But in a conversation which explores deeper matters more often it is marked by pauses, arguments, dead-ends, abrupt changes in theme and by wild inversions. A conversation can include a negotiation about what is to be talked about, and even, a conversation about the conversation. It is streaked through with playfulness and fantasy. The fact that it is a worded phenomenon means, too, that it participates in the illimitable play of language and it is this play which serves partly to create interpretations. For Gadamer words are not signs; they do not have fixed referents (Palmer, 1969: 202). For this reason speech can never master language; it is always capable of being reworked as new significations, previously unconsidered, come to the fore. This is never more so than in poetry, which Gadamer, like Heidegger, sees as a way to reveal Being in new and surprising ways, thereby extending discourse-in-use. For this reason I argue that psychotherapy is closer to poetry than it is to science, as we glimpsed in our examination of therapeutic metaphors.

In the previous section I claimed that skilful therapists are experienced in holding therapeutic conversations. I would also argue that this may in fact be one of the key factors which makes psychotherapy work although I have yet to hear of any process studies which examine this in depth. However that might be I believe that skill in holding therapeutic conversations accounts for six desirable qualities in pursuing both change and emancipation in psychotherapy:

Attentive listening. Therapists not only pay careful

attention to what clients have to say about their affairs but also attend to the reflexive force of their statements, or the way in which the client is documenting the rhetorical-responsive play of the interview.

Attention to power plays. Therapists are aware of the coercive potential for interpretations. In using formulations therapists are aware of two pitfalls. The first is that they can be used dogmatically and, if accepted without question by the client, the result is pedagogy rather than therapy. The second pitfall (or opportunity) is that formulations can only really be put to work if the client can find a use for them. For the latter reason interpretations are subject to the rules of conversation.

Attention to context. This point follows from the one before. Given that therapy takes place under interview conditions the hermeneutically minded therapist is mindful of the fact that the client's statements can be heard as challenging, ironic, disobliging, despairing, etc. That is to say they may have more to do with reactions to the therapeutic gaze rather than with the client herself. Put another way, the therapist's interpretations may need to address the way in which the client is documenting therapy (and, perforce, the therapist's assertions) before continuing further.

Use of empathy. As I have argued before, good inter-pretations occur when the therapist places herself within the horizon of the client. Skilled therapists are adept at providing interpretations that are irre-sistibly linked to things that capture the imagination of the clients, using metaphors, jokes and stories and the like in order to do so.

Changing identities in therapy. Of which the most important is a readiness to step down from the 'expert' position. This is typically required when therapeutic conversations reach an impasse and re-negotiation is required. This, in turn, calls for the therapist to take a back seat for a while and to invite clients to provide more information about their concerns, whether these relate to their dealings in the life-world or to the course of therapy itself, including the interpretations offered to them. At the same time therapists continue to observe the changing voices, positions and roles taken up by the client within the therapeutic interview.

Conversational opportunism. As the conversation unfolds therapists are on the alert for opportunities to weave in fresh material taking advantage of both turns in the conversation and the clients 'readiness' for fresh material. Naturally, this skill requires close attention to non-verbal cues as well as the spoken variety. If this is present then therapists are well-placed to take advantage of those 'right moments' in therapy which will come only once and will never come again, in which a new thought, a new formulation, or a fresh metaphor, will prove inspirational or enlightening.

Versions of therapy on these lines foster what Gadamer refers to as '*Bildung*', one of his favourite terms which has a long history in German philosophy, dating back to the late 18th century, and which is untranslatable from German. It can mean 'self-development', 'cultivation', 'education' or 'maturation'. For Gadamer, psychotherapy is required when the client's capacity for *Bildung* is damaged; the aim of therapy should be to enable the client to recommence the quest for self-completion and thereby to generate a new story about himself which not only accounts for his personal history so far but leads to new possibilities for the future. (Gadamer, 1976: 41).

This type of enquiry leads to the kind of therapeutic change summarised by Goolishian:

> Change in therapy is the dialogical creation of new narrative and therefore the opening of opportunity for new agency. The transformational power of narrative rests in its capacity to re-relate the events of our lives in the context of new and different meaning. We live in and

through the narrative identities that we develop in conversation with each other. The skill of the therapist is the expertise to participate in this process. (Goolishian, 1990: 4).

In moving to what they describe as an explicitly hermeneutic position in psychotherapy Anderson and Goolishian (1992) assert that since the meaning of therapeutic talk is primarily for participants to decide upon what goes on in therapy will always be a function of the communicative actions taken by both parties together. This holds true even where one party 'opts out' of the conversation as this, too, is both a comment on what has just occurred and a type of communicative action in its own right.

This discovery of the meaning of the exchange is facilitated by placing oneself in the horizon of the client and asking, from that position, the question: 'in which context, and for which purposes, does that utterance best make sense?'. Writing in the 1940s Harry Stack Sullivan, a neo-Freudian analyst who anticipated some of the arguments offered here, said that the fundamental question the psychiatrist should always ask was: 'Who is this person and how does he come to be here?' (Sullivan, 1955: 141). On the basis of the argument offered so far we can take this further still and have the therapist ask: Who is this person when she is with me and how does she come to be here in this way?' Questions such as these, as well as conversational strategies which advertise the documentary method being used by the therapist when interpreting the client's speech, work to create dialogues rather than restrictive discourses:

> If one transposes oneself into the position of another with the intent of understanding not the truth of what he is saying, but him, the questions asked in such a conversation are marked by inauthenticity. (Gadamer, 1989: 385)

Therapy which over-relies on method leads to a form of analysis in which therapists and clients are assumed to be interchangeable users of 'invariant technologies, mechanically administered, in which a socially-accredited expert-technician is supposedly able to select a set of specialised techniques to match a diagnosed problem and impersonally apply them' (Kaye, 1994: 37).

By contrast hermeneutic versions of therapy are inherently playful and open-ended. Therapists do not lose sight of their professional role as an inter-preter and guide while avoiding the trap of becoming subsumed by methods, techniques and theories. The poetic quality of speech (defined here as a linguistic capacity for reinventing the world) is acknowledged and utilised while taking care not to let rhetoric become the end of therapy rather than the means.

These recommendations are offered as ideals rather than norms. I am not claiming to follow a 'correct' procedure for psychotherapy with which other approaches can be compared to their disadvantage. The reader will, by now, have realised that such a claim would run counter to the argument of this work. However, moments in which one realises such ideals occur from time to time with the aid of clients and in the extract with which this section concludes, one such moment in therapy is reproduced.

What follows is an extract from the penultimate interview with a 40 year old client whom I shall call 'Paula' complaining originally of free-floating anxiety attacks. These she identified with recent exposure to work-related stress. There were nine interviews altogether. The work of therapy focused on reducing anxiety and on reviewing her perspec-tives on her childhood experiences, along with her attitudes towards her abusers. Progress was such that she was much more tolerant of anxiety by the third interview and free of panic attacks by the fifth. By the sixth interview she was expressing satisfaction with her new-found sense of detachment and with her increasingly assertive relationships with others. While continuing to make therapy available to her if she wished I had before raised the possibility that she might soon terminate therapy. Before this interview (the eighth) I had decided to review our work together and began by asking what progress she had been making since the prior interview. She responded with a narrative concerning her recent experiences at work and her relationship with a bullying manager. She told me that she now saw this person as an object of ridicule rather than fear. The extract begins just here:

1 Paula: And - y'know - if I think of her like that then its - it puts it into uh into the right context I was in a meeting with her the other day - it all looks very good - the power dressing the power speech - but in terms of what she's saying it's all a facade - uh the very thing that she's saying that she's doing like listening to the customer um understanding their problems it's y'know it's crap if you'll pardon the expression she's er she's not listening all she's doing is giving her view of er the event - which may or may not have any relevance at all to erm to the problems that they've got erm - so - I am steadily -

now about what she's saying I just feel dismissive and see it as a non event um - and thinking maybe just leave her to that and go to another employer -

2 Therapist: You know just hearing you telling me about that I came to the feeling that you may have been talking about *us*

3 Paula: [Laughs] I hear what you're saying -

4 Therapist : Um -

5 Paula: Or maybe that's how you feel about therapy -

6 Therapist: I wouldn't like to tell you what I feel about therapy - um - unless you have two hours to spare but - I don't know I don't really know what to say to you there because there was a lot in what you were saying just now that had a lot to do with uh changing your perspective - on things and - what I'd like to know now is where you're going next with that change -

7 Paula: Well - ooh I don't know

A joke (lines 2-3) forms one focus of this exchange in which a statement concerning the client's new-found detachment from her colleague is treated as if it applied to her own therapy. The joke, then, is a disguised formulation which invites the client to consider her current attitude to therapy. She in fact attends to the joke (line 5) with a comment on the attitude of the therapist, itself a reflexive move which (implicitly) addresses the issue of terminating therapy. The joke is an opportunistic use of the narrative in which she has 'seen through' the facade presented by her colleague. As such it is partakes of the peculiarly 'eventful' character of therapeutic conversations in which the flow of talk offers natural openings for a reworking of horizons which may occur once and once only. If not taken the fact that these opportunities are missed could be a sign that therapy is going nowhere in particular.

The metaphorical transferability of her remarks furnishes still another opportunity. She had spoken of her colleague as using 'power speech' in which, while claiming to be listening to customers and 'understanding their problems' she was in reality 'just giving her view of the event'. Applied to the therapeutic setting they work to question whether that was all, by now, that her therapist was doing. Notice that the joke works also to change the topic from workaday problems to therapeutic progress. This is followed up by a request for the client to relate where she might be going next with her changed perspectives on her predicament. The presupposition that 'change' has occurred is borrows support from the background assumption that quite a lot of change had already occurred in prior inter-

views. Her final reply (line 7) exhibits some hesita-
tion as she takes four seconds to pause and respond,
and this is followed by further hesitations. She
continues after this point with a further narrative in
which she switches attention to some family
members with whom she had been conferring on
matters addressed in therapy. However, in the interview which followed she announced her intention
of ceasing therapy on a temporary basis in order to
'see if I can do it on my own'. She also mentioned
that the prior interview had given her much to think
about in making this decision (although no specific
comments were referred to).

There is a further point we can make about the
force of this particular therapeutic intervention and
that is that it deals obliquely with the therapist's
authority. Here we can see this issue addressed indirectly by both therapist and client. The exchange
offers the client the opportunity of applying her
critical insight concerning her manager to the
'power dressing' of therapy. This she takes up by
inviting him to expand on the implications of his
remark. This in turn implies that she has found a
use for therapist's utterance, which is one way that
analysts can test for whether or not a statement has
been taken up and woven into the hermeneutic
fabric.

Working from a discourse-analytic perspective in

which a number of analyses were performed on transcripts of group therapy sessions in Vienna, Wodak has made a similar point in connection with the emancipatory potential of therapeutic talk. With reference to one particular case she remarks:

> We have to conclude that therapeutic discourse, due to its specific setting, the therapeutic technique applied and its isolation from everyday life, allows for small steps towards emancipation. In this case, as in others, the behaviour of the client changes drastically, and she is able to cope with her life in a more satisfactory way. Through an analysis of her power relationship with the therapist, the client...come(s) to terms with other power relationships that she is involved in. Thus power, in this specific context, is not mystified but made explicit and thus refutable. (Wodak, 1996: 168).

The client's relation of some stories about her new-found power in dealing with troublesome people at work is not treated as a diversion but as a resource. It could not have been possible to do this without treating her statements as relevant to the foregoing question I had raised about the course of therapy. Given that her story illustrates her further progress it was utilised, in timely fashion, as an opportunity to transfer her personal power from the workplace to therapy itself. The therapist uses meiosis (lines 19-21: 'you may have been') in order to display the speculative character of this formulation.

6

APPENDIX: PSYCHOTHERAPY AS MORAL INQUIRY

THERAPY AND VIRTUE - THE USE OF METHOD IN THERAPY -
RHETORIC IN THERAPY - FORMULATIONS IN THERAPY -
VOCABULARIES OF MOTIVE - AGENCY AND AUTONOMY -
HERMENEUTICS IN PSYCHOTHERAPY - PSYCHOTHERAPY
AND 'BILDUNG'

I say that virtue is really all about enjoying
yourself, living fully; but of course it is far
from obvious what living fully actually
means.

Terry Eagleton

Take any text book on psychotherapy and it is rare
to find material on morals. It might be thought
strange that a discipline concerned with norms of
conduct, with actions and character, and the difference between the good life and the bad, should be
lacking in this respect but this has been so
throughout its history. Since its inception in the late
nineteenth century psychotherapy has typically

been associated with a science of mental health: a discipline that cuts through the camouflage of common-sense mores and discovers what it is that is really, deeply, wrong with patients. On this scheme citizens are classified not as people who have failed to live up to external moral standards but as 'patients whose behaviour was an uncontrollable manifestation of medical illness' (Cushman, 1995: 67).

Naturally, there are dissenters offering other views of therapy, from R. D. Laing (1965) and Szasz (1972) and the humanistic school forty years ago to narrative therapists and deconstructionist critics today (e.g. White & Epston, 1990; Parker, 1998). However, given the conditions prevailing inside our health services professional accreditation typically centres on the application of therapeutic method. Hence psychotherapists must enter the portals of a training academy which prepares them for accreditation in the designated approach, inculcates learning in the method, disciplines their understanding, and supervises their work. Nor need there be any quarrel with the development of professional standards if by this we mean an education in therapeutic inquiries, adherence to a code of ethics, familiarity with the field, the acquisition of practical experience, and access to professional support. However, the conditions under which therapists are trained, and in which they work, makes of method a terrible temptation insofar as psychotherapy is viewed as a treatment for mental illness.

By therapeutic *method* I mean a blueprint through which the expressions or behaviours of clients are categorised and assessed in terms of some intrapsychic fault. Treatment interventions are then applied with a view to a cure. Such methods are justified by theoretical claims derived from case studies, conceptions of human nature, or psychological experiments. Psychoanalytic method (particularly its Freudian root) is an example of the first; humanistic therapy of the second; and cognitive-behavioural therapy of the third (see Corsini & Wedding (1989) and Nelson-Jones (1996) for an overview). As each of these approaches has evolved then, naturally, they have resorted to all three types of justification, as well as appeals to outcome studies. The application of method in therapy results in discoveries of things like 'distorted cognitions', 'transference', a 'faulty self-object', the 'inner child', 'unfinished gestalts' and 'inauthenticity'. In determining such findings methodic therapists will resort to inference, translation, comparison, analysis, judgement and many other types of interpretive activity.

Therapy and virtue

By *moral* I mean the evaluation of actions or character in terms of good or bad, right and wrong (see the Shorter Oxford English Dictionary for a close definition on these lines). Moral arguments have the further peculiarity that they are reflexively linked to the actions they prescribe (MacIntyre, 1985: 192). Thus to say of oneself that one lacks fortitude or was inconsiderate it follows that one is committed to trying harder at exercising those particular virtues in future. Thus moral reasoning is intricately linked to the pursuit – or the failed pursuit - of virtue. In this way moral activity implies an agent: the bearer of purposive action. And actions may be termed moral when they are linked to the pursuit of virtue. The virtues prescribed are – at bottom - civic in origin and can only make sense to individuals living in speech-communities in which social mores are preserved and transmitted. For it is always 'within some particular community…that we learn or fail to learn the virtues' (MacIntyre, 1998: 87).

The methodic approach to psychotherapy, as I have defined it, is essentially normative. As such it engages its clientele in a search for an ideal self free from defects. On completion of therapy it is hoped that the client will be equipped with fresh virtues. These range from maturity (Perls, 1969: 26), to good judgement (Beck, 1976: 217), self-realisation (Rogers, 1967: 200ff), individuation (Jung, 1986: 210-2), responsibility (Yalom, 1989: 8), authenticity (Rowan, 1983: 62), self control (Berne, 1961: 153ff) and wisdom (van Deurzen-Smith, 1988: 20). Nearly all therapeutic approaches contain both descriptions of the unhealthy self and prescriptions for its restoration. Often the two are linked by opposing terms such as 'repression-knowledge', 'incongruence-wholeness', or 'irrationality-rationality'. Psychotherapy is thus moral insofar as it seeks to develop the virtues inscribed in the approach adopted.

The job of the therapist is to improve the morale of clients by examining and developing the self, a process summarised by Rose in the following terms:

'They [i.e. therapeutic treatments] are characteristically sought when individuals feel unable to bear the obligations of selfhood, or when they are anguished by them. And the rationale of psychotherapies...is to restore to individuals the capacity to function as autonomous beings in the contractual society of the self. Selves unable to operate the imperative of choice are to be restored

through therapy to the status of a choosing
individual.' (Rose, 1990: 227-8).

Rose neatly links notions of the self to the 'contractual society' by which it is defined and delimited.
Discourses of the self are, paradoxically, communal
discourses which prescribe norms of conduct which
must be achieved if clients are to become responsible citizens. That is: I cannot say of myself that I
am wise, truthful or happy without calling upon the
standards which others – including you, the reader
– must confirm. Psychotherapy, while treating the
individual psyche of the client is *ipso facto* concerned
with the moral aims of the community in which
that psyche must function. In a paper published in
this journal three years ago Robinson argued that
therapy is – and should be – a discipline which
alerts its beneficiaries to the 'civic defects or disappointments at the bottom of their various problems'
(Robinson, 1997: 680). He points to the close inter-
play between therapy, moral endeavour and the
civic virtues, a view supported in this essay. Elsewhere, Cushman argues that psychotherapy – in its
methodic guise - cannot escape the moral implications of therapeutic work. By striving to be 'objective' and 'removed from the realm of moral
considerations' (Cushman, 1995: 286-7) therapists
fail to notice that they are in fact reintroducing eval-

uative norms in the language of science. Their practices sustain conceptions of the self which have social and political implications which would be the better for being openly advertised. Cushman argues, as I shall, for a hermeneutic form of therapy in which its moral force can be made more, not less, explicit (op. cit. p294ff).

The use of method in therapeutic interviews

There are, perhaps, as many similarities as differences between therapeutic talk and everyday exchanges. Both exhibit mechanisms through which speakers account for themselves: attributions, justifications, explanations and stories (see Antaki, 1994 for a summary). Thus all conversations assume an unspoken morality in which speakers are sensitive to the possibility that they may be called upon to expand upon, or justify, what has just been said. To some extent psychotherapists rely on these conventions to position clients as providers of accounts which can then be used as the material for therapy (Labov & Fanshel, 1977). Having provided an account the client may be called upon to scrutinise the inner meaning of what has been said in terms of thwarted desires, hidden motives, failed intentions, or misguided purposes. That said, therapeutic interviews have a number of characteristics which, conventionally, distinguish them from other kinds, and these differences make it markedly easier to formalise them. Firstly, then, therapy takes place between an 'expert' practitioner on the one hand and one or more clients on the other. This asymmetry in status imparts a number of distinctive features to the interview. It is the therapist who typically opens and closes the session. It is also the therapist who – as a rule – asks most of the questions. With some exceptions (Ferrara, 1994) it is the client who does most of the talking. This asymmetry is linked to an exposure to the therapist's gaze for it is she who listens to the client's self-disclosure, not the other way around. The client is thus placed in what Foucault refers to as the 'confessional' mode:

> '…a ritual of discourse in which the speaking subject is also the subject of the statement' (Foucault, 1981: 61)

In the realm of traditional psychotherapy and psychiatry it is the therapist's job, as Foucault noted, to decipher what is said by the patient. The inter-pretations of the therapist are designed to reveal the truth about the speaking subject (op. cit. p66-7). In so doing the therapist may be positioned as an expert who can read off what the client has to say in terms of some pre-arranged vocabulary of signs.

Once the asymmetry in roles is understood then the distinguishing features of therapeutic treatments will lie in the assumption that therapists are there to decipher what clients say while clients are there for purposes of self-examination, confession and restoration.

In psychotherapy clients and therapists discuss the client's troubles and their conversation is designed to gather some understanding on this. But since it is a convention in therapy that the client is the final arbiter on claims made about what is happening to him (Labov & Fanshel, 1977: 31), some circumspection must be used where issues of personal responsibility arise. Clients – like other citizens - rely on the assumption (Grice, 1989) that what they have to say is morally and factually adequate. Challenging this assumption leads to interpersonal conflict. For example, in this extract we can read the therapist (Fritz Perls) violating the rule that the client is best equipped to examine her own motives, thereby provoking resistance:

Exhibit 1:

1 Gloria: Ah I want you to help me become more relaxed - yes - I don't want to be so defensive with you I don't like to feel so defensive - um - you're acting like - you're treating me as if I'm stronger

than I am and I want you to - protect me more and be nicer to me -

2 Perls: Are you aware of your smile? You don't believe a word of it

3 Gloria: [laughs] it's true! But I know you're going to pick on me for it -

4 Perls: Sure - you're a bluff - you're a phoney

5 Gloria: Do you believe - you're meaning that seriously?

6 Perls: Yeah - if you say you're afraid and you laugh and you giggle and you squirm - it's it's phoney - you put on a performance for me

7 Gloria: Oh I – resent that – very much!

[Transcript from: Shostrom, 1966)

Lines 2 and 4 contain formulations of the client's actions that label them as insincere. The client's words or non-verbal expressions are thus turned into social actions (in this case to 'disbelieve' or to behave in a 'phoney' way) which can be scrutinised for their moral and practical adequacy. The ensuing discussion will therefore call for self-examination and moral decision. However, an interpretation risks refusal where the therapist assumes superior knowledge about the client's intentions, thereby provoking disputes (as in the prior exhibit). Such disputes could only be avoided where the therapist's authority is accepted unquestioningly. But it could be argued that in such cases therapy has become pedagogy rather than self-transformation.

The rhetoric of therapy

One problem 'expert' therapists are faced with is the difficulty in transiting from conversations about the *reasons* clients give for their predicament to the *causes* of their problem. While the former is a question which is linked to everyday troubles and to personal agency (the lifeworld), the latter (the world of therapeutic discourse) is a matter for expert attention and is linked to theoretical reflections concerning the supposed inner defects that clients have brought with them to therapy. As such therapists reinterpret what client's say into a body of knowledge with predetermined meanings, using rhetoric to do so:

'...theorists, in attempting to represent the open, vague and temporally changing nature of the world as closed, well-defined and orderly, make use of certain textual and rhetorical strategies to construct...*a closed set of intralinguistic references*. They have not, however, appreciated the nature of

the social processes involved in this
achievement. But the fact is, in moving
from an ordinary conversational use of
language to the construction of a
systematic textual discourse, there is a
transition from a reliance on particular,
practical and unique meanings, negotiated
' on the spot' with reference to the
immediate context, to a reliance upon links
with a certain body of already determined
meanings ...' (Shotter, 1993: 25 –
emphasis in original)

When discussing reasons clients may provide anecdotes, metaphors, narratives, descriptions and
complaints. Theories, by contrast, are encumbered
with jargon. Therefore therapists must tread with
care, for too sudden a shift into theory and the
client may (unless she is unusually compliant) resent
the intrusion, but too long a wait and the impatient
therapist becomes embroiled in the client's life-
world, never to emerge again. A compromise solution will be to employ everyday terms as equivalents
for theoretic ones, saving the former for the therapist's clinical notes and discussions with her supervi-
sor. In the hands of such therapists, clients risk
enrolment on a knowledge-mission as well as
subjection to cure. Put another way, the 'Self' about

which knowledge is gathered may have more to do with the therapist's training manual than genuine insight; the 'knowledge' gained may merely reflect a successful induction into the discursive vocabulary employed by the therapist. This rhetorical process of translation in psychotherapy was noted by Szasz (1972: 131-132) nearly fifty years ago. For Szasz, the communications of clients are descriptions of 'problems in living' (Szasz, 1978) that signal distress, express emotion, ask for help, and offer a condensed, indirect, narrative of the circumstances (Szasz, 1972: 128-131). These – in the institutional versions of therapy which Szasz is attacking – are then translated from everyday expressions into discursive codes which reify these situated communications into the outward symptoms of formally treatable disorders. By such means method is inserted into the investigation of the personal and civic origins of the client's distress.

Formulations and the work of therapy

I turn now to one mechanism through which therapists are able to switch the interview from what clients say to the (interpreted) meaning of what they say. It is important to bear in mind that in methodic approaches the client (or, rather, the self) *is* the subject of therapy. Formulations have been shown (Schwartz, 1976; Hak & de Boer, 1995) to be crucial to the work of therapeutic treatment as they are the mechanism by which therapists shift the topic from what clients say to what underlies the statement. It should be borne in mind, however, that formulations can be used in a more dialogic way as shall be explained below when I discuss hermeneutic approaches to therapy.

In the following example a formulation is used in a way that invites the client to perform a self-analysis and come to a decision. The discussion of personal intentions actually constitute an apprenticeship: the client is being shown how to do therapy. Once again, the interpretations offered seek to capitalise on life-world terms used by the client but in a way formulated by the 'expert' voice of the therapist:

Exhibit 2

1 Client: And I just don't know what to do with him. I've cut him way down on money – and I worry about him not having enough money to live on – but I wanted to pressure him to getting a part-time job and get better grades.

2 Therapist: Umm. How much control do you think you have over that?

3 Client: I don't know because um he hasn't called me in three weeks – so I'm not sending him the money 'til he calls me. So – ho-ho – you see? If ya

know he's just – I don't know what to do with him. I thought that may be might be a solution but I don't know. My husband had no solution so I said and we had an argument about it – I said 'I'm not going to argue about it – I'm gonna call Dr. David Visconti and see what he says'

4 Therapist: Yah but ya know there's a whole thing that you're doing here that I'm not sure that you're aware of - to what extent do you believe you're using money to control him?

5 Client: That money will control him?

6 Therapist: No – to what extent are you using money to control him?

7 Client: Oh – not that great much

(Gaik, 1992: 281 – transcript simplified)

In this extract the client is consulting with a radio talk-show therapist concerning the delinquencies of her son, a college student. Note that line 1 is a narrative of attempts to solve the problem. The 'that' to which the therapist's question in line 2 refers is left unspecified in order to focus on the client's motive (her perceived need for 'control'). The client's answer, however, displays an understanding of the question in terms of whether her strategy is *successfully* controlling the son's behaviour. Notice also that she positions the therapist as an expert who may be able to come up with practical advice on how to discipline the son. This is not the reply the therapist wants as his rejoinder in line 4 shows. He reinstates the question, this time using an 'expert' voice to ferret out the motive ('a whole thing you're doing here that I'm not sure you're aware of' – a euphemism, perhaps, for 'denial'). The question is twice qualified with the phrases 'To what extent' and 'do you believe' thus preserving the client's right to adjudicate the answer. But the formulation forcefully shifts the topic (see Potter, 1996: 48-9) and calls for moral self-scrutiny: is the motive to control the son *as a person* rather than just to correct his *behaviour*? But this call is again ignored on line 5 in which the client continues to externalise the motive, thus requiring a second rejoinder phrased in yet more insistent terms. However the client's eventual answer (not 'much') leaves the therapist nowhere to go with this line of inquiry as without the client's take up of the interpretation offered the work of therapy cannot begin. So far her therapeutic apprenticeship has failed.

Vocabularies of motive

The term 'vocabularies of motive' is borrowed from C. Wright Mills' seminal essay (1940) on explanations as types of social action in which respondents use motive talk to explain what they do and anticipate objections. Thus motives are often invoked in everyday interactions in order to explain or justify actions – more specifically actions that have misfired or which were ill-chosen. In treatment interviews, by contrast, motive talk is used by therapists in order to explain the client's actions. And to expedite this they have on hand vocabularies of terms which match the treatment methods they seek to implement. However, the terms remain negotiable to a greater or less degree.

Note that, as shown in the last exhibit, self-examination via the vocabulary of motives will lead not to verifiable truths but to a stake-out of at least two moral positions which the client could take. If the therapist's construction is accepted then the client can continue to use money to control her son, or she can reform her practices in such a way that she can relinquish that control and begin to treat her son as an end in himself. But to do this entails rethinking the nature of motherhood and her occupancy of that particular social role.

The materials of psychotherapy have much to do with the plausible intentions, purposes, motives – conscious or otherwise – that clients have for doing the things they do. And it is here that we enter the realm of moral discourse for, in centring on actions that have gone wrong and the reasons why that might be, we engage in an adjudicative process through which we assess conduct by means of vocabularies of motive, our own and that of others (Pitkin, 1992: 151). Such vocabularies – in therapy – may reflect those used in everyday discourse (loyalties, interests, needs, hopes, commitments, etc) or the technical language of the therapeutic manual (wish-fulfilments, compulsions, low frustration tolerance, self-actualisation, etc) or a combination, or translation, of either. However, the difference between therapeutic vocabularies and everyday ones consists only in the association of the former with formalised practices; ultimately both must result in implied social norms. As therapeutic vocabularies interpenetrate everyday discourse we can expect (some) therapeutic mores to become more and more like everyday ones as they appear in TV soap dramas, advertising and newspaper agony columns (Fairclough, 1992: 98).

Therapeutic knowledge claims are typically embodied in theories of human conduct which explain the causes of therapeutic problems and set out the conditions of their resolution. These theories are replete with jargon. In this connection let us examine the following excerpt from an interview by Albert Ellis:

Exhibit 3

1 Ellis: All right – what's blocking you from getting off your ass?

2 Client: I'm scared!

3 Ellis: Avoid using a word like 'scared' – it's too vague. Now, see if you can answer this question: "If I got off and went out into the world...?' What might happen?'

4 Client: Well I think it's just habit. I've never done it before.

5 Ellis: It's not from habit! You're probably inert from low frustration tolerance.

[Yankura and Dryden, 1990: 102-3]

In line 2 Ellis poses a hypothetical question which, however it is answered, calls for a decision by the client. The use of the words 'if' and 'might' introduce an irrealistic dimension (Gaik, 1992) in which a declared fact (being 'scared') is shown to be a facet – an attribute of the moral universe constructed by the client. Changing the world (into another in which the word 'scared' is avoided and other things 'might happen') will lead implicitly to a change in therapeutic facts about the self. This rhetorical device takes the form of fictional self-talk of the kind the self in this new universe might be expected to use. It remains only for the client to try it on for size and examine its pragmatic value. In line 5 we

notice the eruption of jargon into the argument.
The term 'low frustration tolerance' is peculiar to
the doctrines of Rational-Emotive Behaviour
Therapy (REBT) and features in text-books on the
approach. In formulating her problem in this way
the therapist is extending the client's apprenticeship
in therapy by offering her an entry into the vocabulary of REBT. From hereon further refusals to 'get
off her ass' can be identified as instances of her
disorder. In this way normative standards have now
been erected against which the client's utterances
can be compared and monitored. Once she has
begun to apply this reasoning for herself, to evaluate
her actions against the standards now raised, and to
take corrective action, her induction into REBT is
complete.

The forces against which clients contend may be a
matter of dispute between rival approaches. In
some schools they are unconscious, in some instinctual, in others cognitive. Similarly, the aims of
therapy differ between approaches. Thus a client in
Person-centred therapy may be called upon to get
in touch with a natural self; Kleinians may find that
they have assimilated a good object; while those in
Cognitive therapy may realise a renewed capacity
for rational thought. The reason for the difference
in terminology is that each type of therapy – insofar
as it is offered as a methodic rather than a dialec-

tical approach - is theory-driven. Therapists who non-reflectively follow a method will restrict themselves to a list of virtues and non-virtues, and a corresponding vocabulary of motives, which reflects that theory alone. Thus dogmatic Rogerians (for example) will pursue a morality of self-affirmation and will be concerned with such issues as 'actualization', 'congruence', 'trust', 'growth' and 'acceptance'. Existential therapists of the same stripe may worry about 'self-responsibility', 'openness', 'authenticity', 'conscience' and 'resolution', while some psychoanalysts will concern themselves with 'genitality', 'insight', 'integration', and 'ego-control'.

The professional settings in which psychotherapists operate makes it inevitable that they will be called upon to offer interpretations, give advice or provide instruction. Nor is there, in itself, anything wrong in this. Indeed, without some conceptions of their own to offer therapists may attract complaints that they are short-changing their clients. The fact that a professional may have more interesting interpretations of my conduct to offer than I do myself does not necessarily threaten my autonomy. What is at issue here is the difference between an interpretation offered to an agent with a view to widening her horizons in a way that makes it more likely that informed moral commitments can be developed, and interpretations that merely foster tutelage.

Agency, autonomy and moral choice

If therapists are implicitly engaged in considerations of moral choice by virtue of the professional role they are called upon to fill then (if they are to preserve the ideal of autonomy) the moral dimensions of therapy should be made explicit. Necessarily, moral discussions in therapy will centre on clients' problems in living, their aims and purposes, and the socio-cultural influences with which they have to contend (these may include those which have emerged in the past and which continue to influence them in the present). Such discussions can be profoundly edifying, if not therapeutic:

'Moral discourse is useful, is necessary, because the truths it reveals are by no means obvious. Our responsibilities, the extensions of our cares and commitments, and the implications of our conduct, are not obvious...the self is not obvious to the self. That means both that we do not always see the implications of our own position, who we are; and that we do not always see the reality of our own action, what we have done. In the elaboration of our conduct through speech we disclose and discover, as

> Arendt says, the agent together with the act.' (Pitkin, 1993: 154).

In this passage Pitkin, while discussing moral language games, tells us something interesting about the relationship between morality, agency and the self. Instead of hypothesising that there is a Self which exists prior to any acts or moral choices that it might later embark upon she proposes that the self is in fact formed by those same choices – and by the social cares and commitments which reciprocally spring from them. This is precisely the reverse of therapeutic methods which treat the Self without reference to the network of civic obligations with which it is engaged.

Discarding method – and its paraphernalia of assessment, coding and curative techniques – we would instead be looking *with* the client at their civic defects and disappointments rather than *at* the client's intra-psychic faults. Our approach would rely on active reciprocity rather than expert discernment (see Linge, 1976: xii-xxiii on this hermeneutic point). Formulations can then be used to initiate a dialectic on the unexamined implications of the client's actions in terms of private desires, civic claims, moral choice and autonomous decision. In this mode the knowledge that is unveiled has more to do with the active uncovering of assumptions and limited horizons than with subjectivity. Within the horizon inhabited by the client some purposes may be consciously familiar but others could not be. The therapist's job would be to make it easier for some actions to be recognised and their motives re-appropriated while others are discarded. Either way agency is restored.

Here is an example of what I mean from a tran-script of Family therapy

Exhibit 4

1 Therapist: So if Fred makes that particular face then <u>anything</u> he says means he is tired of your making some mistake?

2 Client: Yeah – well – it sounds kinda -

3 Therapist: What if he makes that face and tells you he has to go to the bathroom. Is that your fault too?

4 Client: Well – no

5 Therapist: Then it's not <u>always</u>?

6 Client: No

9 Therapist: Is it possible that Fred could mean something else and maybe you're just using that face as a way to be hard on yourself?

[Bandler et. al. 1976: 151]

The examination of motives is here carried out by means of critical challenge and re-interpretation: what Fred might mean when he makes a face and – a prompt to the client – the well-springs of self-recrimination which may lead to the juxtaposition of guilt with his frown. The question on line 9 re-interprets the client's actions so that reactions to Fred's facial expressions are formulated in terms of hidden motives of self-blame. Should this formulation of her actions be accepted then the way is open for the client to consider the moral adequacy of her motives in terms of personal and marital obligations. In this way the client is being invited to consider the actions required if she is to mend her relationships. Such an enquiry would lead, perforce, to a restoration of personal agency – to a decision on personal conduct – resulting in a conjugal virtue of some kind.

In the transcript below there is a neat example of a therapist insisting on the exercise of autonomy without at the same time shadowing that autonomy with advice; the therapist prefers to show rather than tell. At the same time, other interpretations of the client's actions are prospected which give the client more credit than he thinks he deserves. In this case the individual is a survivor of an armed robbery describing what were, for him, inadequate responses to the assault. Notice that the dialogue centres on the therapist's attempt to formulate the client's actions as voluntary rather than involuntary. Thus the discussion is about the types of motive at issue as well as the potential virtues that might been exercised.

Exhibit 5

1 Client: They were they were screaming. They were telling everybody 'Get down on the ground or we'll blow your fucking heads off'. Running around, waving their guns.

2 Therapist: Gawd. What did you do?

3 Client: I - I - I didn't say anything.

4 Therapist: What did you do?

5 Client: [Pause] I sort of you know I motioned

6 Therapist: For everyone to get down.

7 Client: Yeah.

8 Therapist: Wow – how did you – I mean how were you able to do that?

9 Client: [shaking head]

10 Therapist: I mean – you know – you say you froze but – I don't know – it sounds more like you kept your cool

11 Client: Hmm

12 Therapist: How did you know that was the right thing to do?

13 Client: [Pauses] I don't know – I never thought of it like that. Maybe maybe um – just instinct.

14 Therapist: You mean – maybe just naturally able to keep your cool?

[Miller et. al. 1997: 153-4]

In this short extract the therapist refers on six occasions to the client's opportunities to exercise personal agency (lines 2, 6, 8, 10, 12 and 14). For the most part the client's response is hardly encouraging; either he did not do (say) anything, or he does not know how he does things, or else his actions are ascribed to impersonal factors ('just instinct'). Yet in each case the therapist's response by prompts for a potential motive (e.g.'protecting others' and 'keeping calm') in everyday terms rather than therapeutic jargon. As noted by Miltenburg and Singer (2000: 519) 'how' questions are more likely to lead to practical moral resolutions than 'why' questions and we see this feature reproduced here.

Hermeneutics in psychotherapy

I turn now to a sketch of hermeneutics that addresses some of the questions explored in this paper. To summarise, these concern the relationship between therapeutic outcomes and the moral aims of the community; the way in which methodic approaches offer a covert moral education; and the question of how therapy can promote agency, autonomy and moral choice. In what follows it is not my intention to offer (what would be impossible) a general interpretation of hermeneutics, or of Gadamer's work. Instead I shall draw upon those hermeneutic resources which are relevant to moral reasoning in psychotherapy. Recent hermeneutic inquiries which have also concerned themselves with psychotherapy as a discipline, moral and other-wise, include Cushman (1995), Eaton (1998), Stan-combe & White (1998), Martin & Dawda (1999), and Polkinghorne (2000).

The term 'hermeneutics' is derived from the Greek for interpretation and, historically, was concerned with the rules and methods required for the effec-tive interpretation of texts. As a discipline its history reaches back to the early nineteenth century and has been applied in philosophy, theology, jurispru-dence, aesthetics and, since Dilthey, to the human sciences (Palmer, 1969; Grondin, 1994). However, the version of hermeneutics which has attracted most attention in recent years amongst social scientists, philosophers and psychotherapists has been that of Gadamer, whose work was defined (by him) as *philosophical hermeneutics* (Grondin, 1994: 1-2). Gadamer's enterprise (hereafter referred to as 'hermeneutics') is primarily concerned with the theory of interpretation: an examination of the conditions that make understanding possible. Following on from Heidegger, whose student he was, Gadamer sought to explicate the way in which interpretations are grounded in the finite, perspectival, culturally-mediated horizons of interpreters. His philosophy seeks to draw limits to interpretation as well as exploring its possibilities. However, hermeneutics itself cannot be a method since it is concerned with discovering the constructions that make interpretations possible and laying them open to examination (Polkinghorne, 2000: 469ff). Hence the account that follows is hermeneutically inspired rather than a proposal for doing therapy.

I have sought to show that interpretive work is pivotal in formulations of motive and that these constitute one avenue through which therapeutic work is accomplished. If this is so then it is advantageous to study what makes an interpretation what it is. In Gadamer's version of hermeneutics interpretation is required when understanding breaks down

(1989: 336). In these situations we seek to restore meaning by discovering the source of our confusion. In doing so we assume that an answer must be possible; our search anticipates completeness (Warnke, 1987: 82ff). In psychotherapy the same principle underlies the therapist's formulations: it is assumed that a complete elucidation of the agent's conscious or unconscious intentions is possible.

At the same time, however, interpretations are limited by the horizon of the interpreter (Gadamer, 1989: 302ff). When we seek to uncover the issue that is addressed by an action we necessarily draw upon our ready-made stock of personal and socio-cultural understandings in order to do so. Therefore interpretations oscillate between certainty and uncertainty: they mediate between our own horizons and that of the other, between the thing to be interpreted and our interpretive resources, between the questions we seek to answer and those the speaker (or text) seeks to answer. Interpretations, therefore, are *always on the way* to understanding (Gadamer, 1981: 105). They can never be complete or definitive and, therefore, the use of therapeutic method requires a three-fold attention to the way it is applied in client interviews, the practical way in which it is taken up by the client, and the pragmatic results which ensue.

Many of Gadamer's writings, particularly his major

work *Truth and Method* (1989) can be read as a critique of the application of method to the human sciences. While recognising that method can yield technical knowledge he attacks the naivete of assuming that such knowledge can be complete, or final, or else can make sense outside the consensus assumptions and practices – often cultural in origin - that make the application of method possible (Warnke, 1987:137). The knowledge claims generated from method can never be total but are marked by the finitude and incompleteness deriving from the horizon of the interpreter and her culturally-effected consciousness (Gadamer, 1989: 340ff).

The defining characteristic of hermeneutic inquiry (its 'universality' as Gadamer would say) is that it seeks to understand a person, a text, or a situation by asking questions which both allow one to understand the other, and to uncover the limited horizon in which those questions have become possible. Method cannot do this because it does not have the reflexive capacity to question itself. If it did so it would surrender to a 'fusion of horizons' (op. cit.) in which its expert pretensions would be extinguished. Hermeneutic inquiry is therefore a process of mediation in which one passes to-and-fro from the I to the Other, from strangeness to familiarity, from part to whole and back again. Thus the restoration (or the enlargement) of understanding devolves upon a dialogue. But because the (horizon of the) self is co-created with (the horizon of) what it is concerned with hermeneutics changes the being of interlocutors in unforeseen ways through discovery. For therapists this will mean an addition to the stock of tacit approaches through which they work with clients; for clients new ways of dissociating themselves from unproductive modes of thought and behaviour and renewed engagements in civic life.

Psychotherapy and 'Bildung'

For Gadamer one mark of a successful course of psychotherapy was that an 'interrupted process of education' (Gadamer, 1976: 41) is retold in a new story uncovered by the client, not by the therapist. In this he refers to the concept of Bildung - '...that by which and through which one is formed becomes completely one's own' (Gadamer, 1989: 11). In English the word is alternately translated by 'education', 'edification' or 'cultivation'. As the definition implies it is linked to an appropriation of the horizon in which the being of the client is formed and, thereafter, to a clearing in which new horizons can emerge. This view of therapy is consistent with Rorty's description of edifying conversations (Rorty, 1980: 357) – a notion itself borrowed from Gadamer - in which individuals seek to discover new and interesting ways to redescribe themselves and their possibilities. In psychotherapy clients are invited to discover their (so far hidden) intentions, build new descriptions of themselves, and then to test the possibilities contained in an alternative moral universe. In edifying conversations that foster *Bildung* the end result is a new narrative of some kind. This takes place as past problems are given a new meaning in terms of a story about how they came to be that way; while the present is shown to be a situation of readiness for new action. This is what is meant by Gadamer's reading of therapy as an 'interrupted process': it is a moment of suspension between past and future before the narrative flow of the client's life can begin anew. And it is narrative which bestows upon clients' actions and motives their moral purpose and sanction (MacIntyre, 1985: 218ff) by situating them within an unfolding, teleological scheme.

The moral action of psychotherapy centres – as I have tried to show – on the therapist's attempt to grasp the motive forces that could explain, or illuminate, the client's actions. Of course, much else goes on in therapeutic talk: descriptions, storytelling, summaries, jokes, ironic remarks, questioning, exhortation, and so on. But interpretive work is linked to questions of agency, motive and moral decision. In accomplishing this vocabularies of motive may be employed to foster understanding and these may be theoretical vocabularies or everyday ones. These, in turn, require clients to perform an evaluation of their conduct which result in a decision to pursue, or disengage from, particular failings and take a new path. Edifying conversations may lead to new insights, actions and encounters with others (Rorty, 1980: 357-365).

In adopting a hermeneutic approach therapists will be concerned with the way in which their interpretations are legitimated. For Gadamer this is a matter for practical philosophy, of which psychotherapy, for him, is one example (Gadamer, 1981: 103ff). Practical philosophy is concerned with the settlement of questions about what is 'the good in human life' (op. cit. p117-118). This, in turn, is linked to the exercise of *phronesis* – the ability to use good judgement in particular cases (Gadamer, 1989: 312; MacIntyre, 1985: 154). Transferred to psychotherapy it relates to practical know-how rather than theoretical formulations. It is joined to the exercise of tact: the ability to find one's way around the complex network of unspoken rules and obligations that form the background to personal decision. Phronetic therapists are always concerned with legitimacy: whether or not they are fostering the client's welfare. For Gadamer legitimacy arises from the facilitation of civic purposes. When an illuminating interpretation leads to fresh conclusions concerning desires, goals and possibilities in relation to the 'social and mental constitution' (Gadamer, 1981: 79) of the client then it becomes possible to engage in practical action which 'code-termines' some new 'communal concerns' (op. cit. p82). Nor are such actions necessarily conformist; they may lead, via a critique of those prejudices which earlier inhibited action, to a challenge to existing conventions.

Conclusion

My major purpose here has been twofold: firstly to illustrate how moral reasoning in psychotherapy works; secondly to show how hermeneutic work can clarify and extend the moral reflections of thera-pists and clients. In doing so I have offered a critique of what I have called 'methodic' approaches to psychotherapy which seek to inter-pret client's in predetermined ways according to the theoretic vocabularies which come with the approach. In doing so I have perhaps not done justice to the many fine therapists who employ methods, singly or in eclectic fashion, as a starting point for their enquiries rather than as a terminus. I have, however, argued that institutional pressures on therapists to justify their practices in terms of scien-tistic claims create an impetus towards the use of formulaic approaches which may lead to a doctrinaire reading of the client's position. Some evidence for this can be gathered from the way in which covert standards are introduced into therapeutic conversations by means of ready-made formulations of the client's spoken interactions. Clients are thereupon enjoined to examine their actions and their hidden motives and to evaluate such motives by comparison with an ideal standard – a self that is fully developed, functional or healthy. Even so, formulations – even those of an initially methodic kind - can be used as a dialectical starting point where they are taken up by clients as illuminating or useful. The more formulations are related to the everyday concerns of the client the more likely such a dialogue will be initiated in ways that lead to productive forms of action and moral decision.

7

REFERENCES

Angus, L. E. (1992). 'Metaphor and the communication interaction in psychotherapy: a multimethodological approach.' In: S. G. Toukmanian & D. L. Rennie (Eds.). *Psychotherapy Process Research*. London: Sage.

Antaki, C. (1994). *Explaining and Arguing*. London: Sage.

Aronson, E. (1976). *The Social Animal*. San Francisco: W H Freeman.

Atkinson, J. M. & Heritage, J. (Eds.) (1984). *Structures of Social Action: Studies in conversation analysis*. Cambridge: Cambridge University Press.

Bakhtin, M. (1986). *Speech Genres and Other Late Essays*. Translated by C. Emerson & M Holquist. Austin: University of Texas Press.

Bandler, R., Grinder, J. & Satir, V. (1976). *Changing with Families*. Palo Alto CA: Science and Behaviour Books.

Bandura, A. (1984). 'Recycling misconceptions of perceived self-efficacy.' *Cognitive Therapy and Research*, 8: 231-255.

Bateson, G. (1972). *Steps to an Ecology of Mind*. New York: Ballantine.

Bergin, A. E. & Lambert, M. J. (1978). 'The evaluation of therapeutic outcomes.' In A. E. Bergin & S. L. Garfield (Eds.), *Handbook of Psychotherapy and Behaviour Change: An Empirical Analysis*. 2nd edition. New York: Wiley.

Bergmann, J. (1992). 'Veiled moralities: notes on discretion in psychiatry.' In P. Drew, & J. C. Heritage, (Eds.), *Talk at Work: Interaction in Institutional Settings*. Cambridge: Cambridge University Press.

Berman, J. & Norton, N. (1985). 'Does professional training make a therapist more effective?' *Psychological Bulletin*, 98: 401-7.

Bialostosky, D. H. (1995). 'Antilogics, dialogics, and sophistic social psychology: Michael Billig's reinvention of Bakhtin from Protagorean rhetoric.' In: S. Mailloux (Ed.). *Rhetoric, Sophistry and Pragmatism*. Cambridge: Cambridge University Press.

Caputo, J. D. (2018). *Hermeneutics: Facts and Interpretation in the Age of Information*. London: Penguin Books Ltd.

Clare, A. (1976). *Psychiatry in Dissent: Controversial issues in thought and practice*. 2nd Edition. London: Tavistock.

Clarkson, P. (1989). *Gestalt Counselling in Action*. London: Sage.

Coombs, G. & Freedman, J. (1990). *Symbol, Story & Ceremony*. New York: W. W. Norton.

Cooper. D. E. (1986). *Metaphor*. Oxford: Blackwell.

Corsini, R.J., & Wedding, D. (Eds.). (1989). *Current psychotherapies* (4th Ed.) Itasca IL: Peacock.

Cushman, P. (1995). *Constructing the self, constructing America: A cultural history of psychotherapy*. New York: Addison-Wesley.

Davidson, D. (1978). 'What metaphors mean.' In: S. Sacks (Ed.) *On Metaphor*. Chicago: University of Chicago Press.

Derrida, J. (1981). *Positions*. Translated and annotated by A. Bass. London: The Athlone Press.

Dryden, W. (1991). *A Dialogue with Arnold Lazarus: 'It Depends'*. Milton Keynes: Open University Press.

Dryden, W. & Gordon, J. (1990). *What is Rational-*

Emotive Therapy? Loughton: Gale Centre Publications.

Durham, R., Chambers, J., Power, K., Sharp, D., Macdonald, R., Major, K., Dow, M. & Gumley, A. (2005), Long-term outcome of cognitive behaviour therapy clinical trials in central Scotland. *Health Technology Assessment*, vol. 9, no. 42, pp. 1-4.

Eaton, J. (1998). Gadamer: Psychotherapy as conversation. *European Journal of Psychotherapy, Counselling & Health*, 1, 421-433.

Eaton, J. (2002). Psychotherapy and moral enquiry. *Theory & Psychology*, 12, 367-386

Eliot, T. S. (1950). *The Cocktail Party*. London: Faber.

Ellenberger, H. F. (1994). *The Discovery of the Unconscious*. London: Fontana.

Ellis, A. (1989). 'Rational-Emotive therapy.' In: *Current Psychotherapies*. R.J. Corsini & D. Wedding (Eds.). 4th edition. Itasca IL: F. E. Peacock.

Ellis, A. (1991). *Reason and Emotion in Psychotherapy*. New York: Citadel Press.

Epston, D. (1993). 'Internalizing discourses versus externalizing discourses.' In S. Gilligan, & R. Price, (Eds.). *Therapeutic Conversations*. New York: W. W. Norton.

Eysenck, H. J. (1952). 'The effects of psychotherapy: an evaluation.' *Journal of Consulting Psychology*, 16: 319-324.

Eysenck, H. J. (1966). *The Effects of Psychotherapy*. New York: International Science Press.

Eysenck. H. J. (1992). 'The outcome problem in psychotherapy.' In W. Dryden & C. Feltham (Eds.). *Psychotherapy and its Discontents*. Milton Keynes: Open University Press.

Fairclough, N. (1989). *Language and Power*. London: Longman.

Fairclough, N. (1992). *Discourse and Social Change*. Cambridge: Polity Press.

Ferrara, K. W. (1994). *Therapeutic Ways with Words*. Oxford: Oxford University Press.

Fiedler, F. E. (1950). 'A comparison of therapeutic relations in psychoanalytic, non-directive and Adlerian therapy.' *Journal of Consulting Psychology*, 14: 436-455.

Foucault, M. (1981). *The History of Sexuality Volume I: An introduction*. Translated by R. Hurley. London: Pelican.

Frank, J. (1973). *Persuasion and Healing*. 2nd Edition. Baltimore MD: Johns Hopkins University Press.

Freud, S. (1895). *Project for a Scientific Psychology*. *The Standard Edition of the Complete Psychological Works of Sigmund Freud* (SE: Volume I). Edited by J. Strachey. London: Hogarth Press and the Institute of Psychoanalysis.

Freud, S. (1912). *Recommendations to Physicians Practising Psychoanalysis*. SE (Volume XII).

Gadamer, H-G. (1976). *Philosophical Hermeneutics*. Translated and edited by D. Linge. Berkeley CA: University of California Press.

Gadamer, H-G. (1983). *Reason in the Age of Science*. Translated by F. G. Lawrence. Cambridge MA: MIT Press.

Gadamer, H-G. (1989). *Truth and Method*. 2nd edition. Translation revised by J. Weinsheimer and D. Marshall. London: Sheed & Ward.

Gaik, F. (1992). 'Radio talk-show therapy and the pragmatics of possible worlds.' In: A. Duranti & C. Goodwin (Eds.). *Rethinking Context: Language as an interactive phenomenon*. Cambridge: Cambridge University Press.

Garfield, S. L. (1980). *Psychotherapy: An Eclectic Approach*. New York: Wiley.

Garfinkel, H. (1984). *Studies in Ethnomethodology*. Cambridge: Polity Press.

Gay, P. (1988). *Freud: A life for our time*. London: J. M. Dent.

Gellner, E. (1993). *The Psychoanalytic Movement*. 2nd Edition. London: Fontana.

Gellner, E. (1992). 'Psychoanalysis, social role & testability.' In: W. Dryden & C. Feltham (Eds.). *Psychotherapy and its Discontents*. Milton Keynes: Open University Press.

Gergen, K. J. & Gergen, M. M. (1986). 'Narrative form and the construction of psychological science.' In: T. Sarbin (Ed.) *Narrative Psychology: The storied nature of human conduct*. New York: Praeger.

Gergen, K. J. & Gergen, M. M. (1987). 'Narratives of friendship.' In: R. Burnett, P McGhee & D. Clarke (Eds.). *Accounting for relationships*. London: Methuen.

Giannitrapain, D. (1987). *Mutative Metaphors in Psychotherapy*. London: Tavistock.

Gilbert, G. N. & Mulkay, M. (1984). *Opening Pandora's Box: A sociological analysis of scientists' discourse*. Cambridge: Cambridge University Press.

Gordon, D. (1978). *Therapeutic Metaphor*. Cupertino CA.: Meta Publications.

Goolishian, H. A. (1990). 'Therapy as a linguistic

system: hermeneutics, narrative and meaning.' *The Family Psychologist*, 6: 14-45.

Grice, P. (1989). *Studies in the Way of Words*. Cambridge MA: Harvard University Press.

Grondin, J. (1994). *Introduction to Philosophical Hermeneutics*. (J. Weinsheimer, Trans.). New Haven CT: Yale University Press.

Grunbaum, A. (1984). *The Foundations of Psychoanalysis: A Philosophical Critique*. Berkeley CA: University of California Press.

Hak, T. & de Boer, F. (1995). 'Professional interpretation of talk in the initial interview.' In J. Siegfried, (Ed.). *Therapeutic and Everyday Discourse as Behaviour Change: Towards a micro-analysis in psychotherapy process research*. Norwood NJ: Ablex Publishing Corporation.

Haley, J. (1976). *Problem-Solving Therapy*. New York: Harper Row.

Harper, R. (1959). *Psychoanalysis and Psychotherapy: 36 Systems*. Englewood Cliff NJ: Prentice-Hall.

Hattie, J., Sharpley, C. and Rogers, H. (1984). 'Comparative effectiveness of professional and paraprofessional helpers.' *Psychological Bulletin*, 95: 534-41.

Heidegger, M. (1988). *Ontology: The hermeneutics of*

facticity. Translated by J. van Buren. Bloomington: Indiana University Press.

Herink, R. (Ed.).(1980). *The Psychotherapy Handbook*. New York: Meridian Books.

Heritage, J. C. (1984). *Garfinkel and Ethnomethodology*. Cambridge: Polity Press.

Hobson R. F. (1985). *Forms of Feelings*. London: Tavistock.

Holmes, J. (1983). 'The functions of tag questions.' *English Language Research Journal*, 3, 40-65.

Howarth, I. (1989). 'Psychotherapy: who benefits?' *The Psychologist*, 2, 4: 149-52.

Hutton, P. H. (1988). 'Foucault, Freud and the technologies of the self.' In: *Technologies of the Self*. Edited by L. H. Martin, H. Gutman & P. H. Hutton. London: Tavistock.

Jung, C. G. (1986). *Jung: The Essential Writings*. London: Fontana.

Kaye, J. (1995). 'Psychotherapeutic discourse: notes on a prospective frame.' In: J. Siegfried, (Ed.). *Therapeutic and Everyday Discourse as Behaviour Change: Towards a micro-analysis in psychotherapy process research*. Norwood NJ: Ablex Publishing Corporation.

Kline, P. (1992). 'Problems of methodology in

studies of psychotherapy.' In: W. Dryden & C. Feltham (Eds.). *Psychotherapy and its Discontents*. Milton Keynes: Open University Press.

Kovel, J. (1976). *A Complete Guide to Therapy: From psychoanalysis to behaviour modification*. London: Pelican.

Labov, W. & Fanshel, D. (1977). *Therapeutic Discourse: Psychotherapy as conversation*. New York: Academic Press.

Laing, R. D. (1965). *The Divided Self*. London: Pelican.

Lazarus, A. A. (1989a). *The Practice of Multimodal Therapy*. Baltimore MD: Johns Hopkins University Press.

Lazarus, A. A. (1989b). Multimodal therapy. In: *Current Psychotherapies*. 4th edition. R. J. Corsini & D. Wedding (Eds.). Ithaca IL: F. E. Peacock.

Lee, J. R. E. (1995). 'The trouble is nobody listens.' In: J. Siegfried, (Ed.). *Therapeutic and Everyday Discourse as Behaviour Change: Towards a micro-analysis in psychotherapy process research*. Norwood NJ: Ablex Publishing Corporation.

Levinson, S. C. (1983). *Pragmatics*. Cambridge: Cambridge University Press.

Lichtenberg, G. C. (1990). *Aphorisms*. Translated. by R.J. Hollingdale. London: Penguin.

Linge, D.E. (1976). Editor's introduction. In. H-G. Gadamer, *Philosophical Hermeneutics*. Translated and edited by D. Linge. Berkeley CA: University of California Press.

Luborsky, L. L. & Singer, B. (1975). 'Comparative studies of psychotherapies: is it true that 'everyone has won and all must have prizes'?' *Archives of General Psychiatry*, 32: 995-1008.

Luborsky, L. L. & Spence, D. (1978). 'Quantitative research on psychoanalytic psychotherapy.' In A. E. Bergin & S. L. Garfield (Eds.), *Handbook of Psychotherapy and Behaviour Change: An Empirical Analysis*. 2nd edition. New York: Wiley.

Luborsky, L. L., McLellan, A. T., Woody, G. E., O'Brien, E. P. & Auerbach, A. (1985). 'Therapist success and its determinants.' *Archives of General Psychiatry*, 42: 602-611.

MacIntyre, A. (1985). *After Virtue*. London: Duckworth.

MacIntyre, A. (1998). *The MacIntyre Reader*. Cambridge: Polity.

Martin, J. & Dawda, D. (1999). Beyond empathy: A hermeneutically inspired inquiry into interpersonal

understanding   in   psychotherapy.   *Theory   &
Psychology*, 9, 459-581

Macdonnell, D. (1986). *Theories of Discourse: An Introduction*. Oxford: Basil Blackwell.

Miller, S.D., Duncan, B.L., & Hubble, M.A. (1997).
Escape from Babel. New York: Norton.

Mills, C.W. (1940). Situated actions and vocabularies
of motive. *American Sociological Review*, 5, 904-913

Miltenburg, R. & Singer, E. (2000). A concept
becomes a passion: Moral commitment and the
affective development of the survivors of child
abuse. *Theory & Psychology*, 10, 503-526

Morrow-Bradley, C. & Elliott, R. (1986). 'Utilization
of psychotherapy research by practising psychotherapists.' *The American Psychologist*, 41, No. 2: 188-197.

Nelson-Jones, R. (1995). *The Theory and Practice of
Counselling*. 2nd Edition. London: Cassell.

Oatley, K. (1984). *Selves in Relation: An introduction to
psychotherapy and groups*. London: Methuen.

Palmer, R. (1969). *Hermeneutics: Interpretation theory in
Schleiermacher, Dilthey, Heidegger and Gadamer*. Evanston
IL.: Northwestern University Press.

Parker, I. (1998). Constructing and deconstructing

psychotherapeutic discourse. *European Journal of Psychotherapy, Counselling and Health.*, 1, 65-78

Perls, F. S. (1969). *Gestalt Therapy Verbatim.* Compiled and edited by J. Stevens. Moab Utah: Real People Press.

Perls, F. S., Hefferline, R. F., & Goodman, P. (1973). *Gestalt Therapy.* London: Pelican.

Pitkin, H.F. (1993). *Wittgenstein and Justice.* Berkeley: University of California Press.

Polkinghorne, D.E. (2000). Psychological enquiry and the pragmatic and hermeneutic traditions. *Theory & Psychology*, 10, 453-479

Potter, J. & Wetherell, M. (1987). *Discourse and Social Psychology.* London: Sage.

Potter, J. (1996a). 'Right and wrong footing.' In: *Theory & Psychology*, 6, 31-39.

Potter, J. (1996b). *Representing Reality.* London: Sage Publications

Rachman, S. J. & Wilson, G. T. (1980). *The Effects of Psychological Therapy.* (2nd edition). New York: Pergamon Press

Reich, W. (1950). *Character Analysis.* 3rd Edition. Trans: T. Wolfe. London: Vision Press.

Rieff, P. (1966). *The Rise of The Therapeutic*. London: Chatto & Windus.

Robinson, D.N. (1997). Therapy as theory and civics. *Theory & Psychology*, 7, 657-681

Rogers, C. R. (1967). *On Becoming A Person: A therapist's view of psychotherapy*. London: Constable.

Rogers, C. R. (1986). 'Client-centred therapy.' In I. Kutash & A. Wolf (Eds.), *Theory and Technique in the Practice of Modern Therapies*. San Francisco: Jossey-Bass.

Rogers, C. R. (1990). *The Carl Rogers Reader*. Edited by H. Kirschenbaum & V. L. Henderson. London: Constable.

Rose, N. (1990). *Governing the Soul: The shaping of the private self*. London: Routledge.

Rowan, J. (1992). 'Response'. In: W. Dryden & C. Feltham (Eds.). *Psychotherapy and its Discontents*. Milton Keynes: Open University Press.

Rycroft, C. (1968). 'Introduction: causes and meaning.' In: C. Rycroft, G. Gorer, A Storr, J. Wren-Lewis, P. Lomas. *Psychoanalysis Observed*. Harmondsworth: Penguin

Rycroft, C. (1971). Reich. Glasgow: Fontana.

Schwartz, H. (1976). 'On recognizing mistakes: a

case of practical reasoning in psychotherapy.' *Philosophy of Social Science*, 6, 55-73

Shapiro, D. A. (1985). 'Recent applications of meta-analysis in clinical research.' *Clinical Psychological Review*, 5, 13-34.

Shapiro, D. A., Barkham, M., Hardy, G. E. & Morrison, L. A. (1990). 'The second Sheffield psychotherapy project: rationale, design and preliminary outcome data.' *British Journal of Medical Psychology*, 63, 97-108.

Shostrom, E. (1966). *Three Approaches to Psychotherapy* [Film]. Santa Ana CA: Psychological Films.

Shotter, J. (1993). *Conversational Realities*. London: Sage.

Sloane, R. B., Staples, F. R., Cristol, A. H., Yorkston, N. J., & Whipple, K. (1975). *Psychotherapy Vs. Behaviour Therapy*. Cambridge MA: Harvard University Press.

Smail. D. (1983). 'Psychotherapy and psychology.' In: D. Pilgrim (Ed.), *Psychology and Psychotherapy: Current trends and issues*. London: Routledge.

Smith, M. L., Glass, G. V. & Miller, T. I. (1980). *The Benefits of Psychotherapy*. Baltimore MD: Johns Hopkins University Press.

Soyland, A. J. (1994). *Psychology as Metaphor*. London: Sage.

Spence, D. (1982). *Narrative Truth and Historical Truth: Meaning and interpretation in psychoanalysis*. New York: W. W. Norton.

Spence, D. (1986). 'Narrative smoothing & clinical wisdom.' In: T. R. Sarbin, (Ed.). *Narrative Psychology: The storied nature of human conduct*. New York: Praeger.

Stancombe, J., & White, S. (1998). Psychotherapy without foundations? Hermeneutics, discourse and the end of certainty. *Theory & Psychology*, 8, 579-599

Stiles, W. B., Shapiro, D. A., & Elliott, R. (1986). 'Are all psychotherapies equivalent?' *American Psychologist*, 41, 165-80.

Storr, A. (1979). *The Art of Psychotherapy*. London: Secker & Warburg.

Sullivan, H. S. (1953). *The Interpersonal Theory of Psychiatry*. New York: W. W. Norton.

Sullivan, H. S. (1955). *The Psychiatric Interview*. London: Tavistock Publications.

Sulloway, F. J. (1980). *Freud, Biologist of the Mind*. London: Fontana.

Szasz, T. (1972). *The Myth of Mental Illness.* London: Paladin Books.

Szasz, T. (1973). *Ideology and Insanity.* London: Pelican.

Szasz, T. (1978). *The Myth of Psychotherapy.* New York: Doubleday Anchor.

Todorov, T. (1984). *Mikhail Bakhtin: The ideological principle.* Translated by W. Godzich. Minneapolis: University of Minnesota Press.

Tolstoy, L. (1978). *War and Peace.* Translated by R. Edmonds. Harmondsworth: Penguin.

Van Deurzen, E. (1988). *Existential counselling in practice.* London: Sage.

Warnke, G. (1987). *Gadamer: Hermeneutics, tradition and reason.* Cambridge: Polity.

Wilde, O. (1954). *Plays.* Harmondsworth: Penguin.

Wilkins, W. (1984). 'Psychotherapy: the powerful placebo.' *Journal of Consulting and Clinical Psychology,* 52, 570-573.

Winefield, H. R., Bassett, D. L., Chandler, M. A., & Proske, I. (1987). 'Process in psychotherapy as decreasing asymmetry between patient and therapist: Evidence from the verbal interaction.' *American Journal of Psychotherapy,* 41, 117-26.

Winefield, H. R., Chandler, M. A., & Bassett, D. L. (1989). 'Tag questions and powerfulness: Quantitative and qualitative analyses of a course of psychotherapy.' *Language in Society*, 18, 77-86.

Wittgenstein, L. (1966). *Lectures and Conversations on Aesthetics, Psychology and Religious Belief*. Edited by C. Barrett. Oxford: Basil Blackwell.

Wodak, R. (1996). *Disorders of Discourse*. Harlow: Addison Wesley Longman.

Wolpe, J. (1958). *Psychotherapy by Reciprocal Inhibition*. Stanford CA: Stanford University Press

Wolpe, J. (1973). *The Practice of Behaviour Therapy*. Oxford: Pergamon Press.

Yankura, J. & Dryden, W. (1990). *Doing RET: Albert Ellis in Action*. New York: Springer.

Yankura, J. & Dryden, W. (1994). *Albert Ellis*. London: Sage.

INDEX

. . .

.   .   .

www.ingramcontent.com/pod-product-compliance
Lightning Source LLC
Chambersburg PA
CBHW031119020426
42333CB00012B/154